Norse Magic and Asatru

An Essential Guide to Norse Divination, Elder Futhark Runes, Paganism, and Heathenry for Beginners

Your Free Gift (only available for a limited time)

Thanks for getting this book! If you want to learn more about various spirituality topics, then join Mari Silva's community and get a free guided meditation MP3 for awakening your third eye. This guided meditation mp3 is designed to open and strengthen ones third eye so you can experience a higher state of consciousness. Simply visit the link below the image to get started.

https://spiritualityspot.com/meditation

Contents

Part 1: Norse Magic for Beginners

The Ultimate Guide to Norse Divination, Reading Elder Futhark Runes, and Spells

Introduction

Do you love mythology? One topic you may find interesting is Norse mythology, particularly their ancient beliefs and the magical practices used in Norse witchcraft. If you have a strong interest in learning this magic, remember that you first need a solid foundation of the Nordic principles and beliefs. You have to build your knowledge about such tenets and beliefs to apply them when practicing Norse magic.

Few other cultures can compare with the intricacies and mystery surrounding the Norse. Their mythology is so vast and yet vague simultaneously. It is this unknown factor - the mystery - that makes people want to learn more about it. Of all the subjects covered about the ancient Norsemen, their divination and magical practices are among the most interesting.

Most people first learned about the ancient Norse through the mythologies surrounding the Asgardian gods they used to worship. It is all thanks to them getting the mainstream treatment in television, movies, comic books, and video games, but Norse magic involves more than just that.

It is where you will find this book, Norse Magic for Beginners: The Ultimate Guide to Norse Divination, Reading Elder Futhark Runes, and Spells, useful. This book will serve as your ultimate source of information regarding Norse magic. If you are a beginner, this book is what you have been looking for. It is easy to understand and contains updated information about Norse mythology and magic.

Even complex terms are explained simply, so those who have no idea what Norse is can easily grasp its meaning. This book will teach you about the supernatural practices that the ancient Norse people used to practice, like divination, rune casting, and how to cast an assortment of spells. This book is written so the whole learning process will become more fun and exciting.

I hope this book will quell your curiosity toward the Norse and their mysterious religious practices. I hope it will also inspire you to further your research about the Norse people and their colorful history.

Chapter 1: Following the Footsteps of the Vikings

Every time you hear the word "Norse," the Vikings may the first people that will most likely come to mind. Before the European colonizers forced them into Christianity, the Vikings and other Scandinavian tribes had their own pagan culture and religion. Thankfully, some ancient texts and practices survived the purge of the colonizers, and people are rediscovering them today.

The Norse, also called the Germanic religion, is polytheistic. It means that the people believed in many gods and goddesses - with each having different areas of expertise. There are gods/goddesses of love, agriculture, war, and many other aspects. Back then, who you worshipped would largely depend on your vocation or the community where you belonged.

The Creation of the World

According to the Norse (Old Germanic) pagan beliefs, the gods and all the beings who are in the Nine Worlds originated from a singular being, which is the giant known as Ymir, otherwise called Aurgelmir, Brimir, or Blainn. Legends say that Ymir was born from the water droplet that formed when the ice from Niflheim met the heat from Muspelheim.

Thanks to his hermaphroditic body, Ymir birthed the first generation of the first gods, goddesses, and other mythical creatures who would then bear the succeeding generations.

Among the younger gods that came from Ymir were the brothers Ve, Vili, and Odin. It was in their hands where the great giant fell. These three Norse gods then created the Earth, which they called Midgard. It is the realm that bridges the gap between the land of the gods known as Asgard and the land of the dead, which is Hel.

The Pantheon of Norse Gods

The Norse gods are of three classifications:

- **The Aesir** - These are the gods of the tribes or clans. They represent kingship, craft, and order, among many other things, and Odin and Thor are two of the gods in this classification. These Germanic gods are residents of the realm known as Asgard.

- **The Vanir** - These are the gods of the Earth and the forces of nature who are also the deities of fertility. Among them are Freyr and Freya.

- **The Jotnar** - These are the giants that occupy the realms of Jotunheim and Muspelheim. These beings are in a constant war with the Asgardians, which is why they represent chaos and destruction.

Most people intensely worship four of the deities and mythical creatures populating the nine realms. They are:

• **Odin** - Also known as Woden, Odin is the All-Father, the ruler of all the Aesir and Vanir. He is the most revered but also the most mysterious of all the Norse gods. Most people portray him as a haggard wanderer, relentlessly seeking knowledge despite ruling all Asgard.

Don't be fooled with Odin's always benevolent portrayal in mass media, though, as he is not perfect. He also has a sinister side to him. Odin is depicted as the epitome of battle frenzy. He has provoked countless wars.

• **Thor** - Undoubtedly, Thor is the most well-known of all the Germanic Norse gods, and most of his fame came from modern comics, cartoons, and movies, but modern-day Thor does not resemble his Norse mythology counterpart. Aside from being gruff and wielding the magical hammer Mjolnir, the resemblances stop there.

The actual Thor is a redhead with red eyes, and he rides a chariot pulled by two giant goats. Aside from being the defender of Asgard and the god of the sky and thunder, Thor is also the god of agriculture, fertility, and hallowing.

• **Freyr** - Probably one of the most beloved of all the Norse gods along with his twin sister Freya, Freyr has a unique origin. Unlike most of the other Germanic gods, Freyr came from the Vanir tribe.

Usually portrayed as a large and brawny man with long flowing hair, the Norse hailed him as the topmost god with fertility, and in agriculture, harvests, wealth, peace, and sexual virility. Since the ancient Norse relied heavily on agriculture, many worship Freyr hoping to have a bountiful harvest all the time.

- **Freya/Freyja** – She is the twin sister of Freyr and the Norse goddess of beauty and love. She is also famous for being the goddess of fate and destiny. She and her twin brother Freyr became honorary members of the Aesir after the tribal war between them and the Vanir. According to the Norse religion, Freya could tinker with people's destinies.

Religious Practices

The ancient people who practiced the Germanic pagan religion often held their rituals in or near bodies of water like lakes, bogs, and marshes. They believed that such places are sacred and can let the mortals contact the divine. It is the reason archaeologists find numerous wooden figures depicting people with strongly emphasized sexual features, suggesting that they were offerings to the Norse pagan gods of fertility.

Sacrifices were fundamental elements of Norse/Germanic religion. The ancient people believed that destroying or sending the sacrifice in a place where humans cannot access them is a surefire way for them to reach their intended deities. The ritual burning or throwing of sacrificial objects into lakes became frequent. Festivals also frequently accompanied these rituals – with them all involving copious amounts of eating and drinking.

Often, carved wooden figurines were used for sacrifice, but there were also times when people were offered to the gods by weighing them down using stones and throwing them into boggy marshes. Most of the time, the victims were purported to be witches who brought misfortune to their community. Peat bogs were the preferred sacrificial altar of sorts because the body would not dissolve and get sent to the other world. Instead, it was preserved forever in a state in-between our world and the other world.

At other times, the Norse people would offer their beloved weapons to their gods. Oddly enough, you will not find human remains in the places where weapons are offered up to the gods. Often, the weapons used for sacrifice came from the Norse people's slain enemies, and these were usually sent to Odin.

Modern Germanic/Norse Religion and Practices

If you think that the Norse religion is long gone, then you will be surprised to know that it still exists up to today. You can still find many groups of people around the world but mostly concentrated within Europe and in the Scandinavian isles, who practice a modern form of the pagan religion. They unironically call the practice Heathenry.

Heathens, pertaining to those who practice Heathenry, used to be a derogatory term, and it still is actually. It pertains to the uncivilized societies that have not been converted to Christianity. Heathenry is now a form of a new religious movement that aims to reconstruct the pre-Christian belief systems of the Norse/Germanic tribes and apply them to modern times. Practitioners of Heathenry seek to revive the ancient belief systems using whatever surviving historical source materials they can muster.

Just like the ancient Germanic religion, Heathenry has not unanimously accepted theology. Today's form of Heathenry is polytheistic, just like the ancient pagan religion. It also features a pantheon of gods and goddesses, the same ones that the early Germanic tribes used to worship.

Unlike Christianity, the gods and goddesses of Heathenry are not perfect, omnipotent, and omnipresent. They think of them as having their own strengths and weaknesses. They believe that their gods will one day die like what befell Baldr in Norse mythology.

What is Asatro?

Speaking of the modern Norse religion, it is important to learn about what Asatro is. Asatro refers to the modern term used to define the act of worshipping Norse gods – the ones practiced by the old believers thousands of years ago. This concept does not just focus on the gods. It also aims to worship ancestors and giants. The term is relatively modern and gained recognition only during the 19th century.

The Asatro is divided into kindreds. These refer to local worship groups. Also called stead or garth, kindreds could either be affiliated or not to a national organization. They also consist of hearths, individuals, or families. Kindred members tend to become related through marriage or blood.

Asatro, as the modern version of the Norse religion, also runs based on nine important virtues. Composed of ethical and moral standards derived from various literary and historical sources, Asatro works based on these nine noble virtues that also form a huge part of Norse paganism:

- **Courage** - It encompasses both moral and physical courage. The courage mentioned here is the ability to stand up for your beliefs, especially in terms of what is just and right. This means you have your own persona and are not easily swayed by popular opinion.

- **Truth** - This virtue covers different kinds of truth, including actual and spiritual truth. It is a powerful virtue, which serves as a reminder to everybody of the importance of speaking the truth instead of talking based on what others want to hear.

- **Honor** - It covers your moral compass and reputation. This virtue makes you remember how important it is to be mindful of your words, reputation, and deeds as all those can outlive your human body. This means that people will remember the way you live your life for quite a long time.

- **Fidelity** - This virtue is also another one that people will remember you by. It is all about staying true not only to the Gods you know but also to your kinsmen, community, and spouse. It also revolves around loyalty. This means that letting down a friend, your Gods, or a kindred member also signifies that you turn your back on the whole community and its beliefs and principles.

- **Discipline** - This noble virtue is all about upholding your honor and your other virtues willingly. Note that to be just and ethical, you need to build discipline - strong mental discipline, to be exact. There, your willingness also matters since it is your choice to uphold the virtues you believe in.

- **Hospitality** - The hospitality virtue is not just the simple act of accepting guests with open arms. It is also the way you treat others. You must treat the surrounding people with respect and be willing to be part of your community.

- **Industriousness** - This virtue signifies how important it is to work hard to attain your goals. It requires you to implement hard work in all the things you intend to do, as you owe this not only to yourself but also to the Gods, your family, and your community.

- **Self-Reliance** - This is the eighth noble virtue you must develop to practice Asatro. It is all about your ability to take care of yourself and maintain strong relationships with the deity. Note that while honoring the gods is extremely important, you should also not forget to give both your mind and body the care they need. In Asatro, you must look for the balance between doing for yourself and doing for others.

- **Perseverance** – last, there is this noble virtue called perseverance. Here, you will need to push onward regardless of all the obstacles that get in your way. If you built this vital virtue, then you would be capable of rising even if you were dealing with defeat. Your perseverance will also let you learn and achieve growth, even if you have committed mistakes and made poor choices along the way.

All these virtues are also among those that most modern Norse believers live by.

Practices of Heathenry

Heathenry celebrates two main rites called blōt and symbel (pronounced as sumble). Practitioners of Heathenry would often hold feasts based around these two main rites, like rites of passage, rites that honor a particular god or gods, and many other forms of celebration.

Originally, a blōt would include the ritual sacrifice of one or more animals to gain the favor of one or more gods or honor their ancestors. After the ritual sacrifice, a feast will be held, allowing the participants of the rite to partake of the meat of the sacrificed animal. Usually, a blōt occurs if the people wish for a particular purpose, like peace, good weather, bountiful crops, or victory.

A modern blōt no longer includes an animal sacrifice, as most people perceive it as too inhumane. It now centers upon offering food, drink, or any other items to the gods, but there will still be a feast after finishing the rite. For outdoor blōts, the items for sacrifice are often thrown into a raging bonfire. But for an indoor blōt, the participants reserve a place setting for the god or ancestor they wish to honor.

A symbel is a rite where there is a drinking horn or two filled with mead or any appropriate alcoholic beverage. After having the drinks blessed and sanctified according to Heathenistic practices, the practitioners will pass the horns around, and each will take a drink. The first round of toasts is usually offered to the gods, the second round for the ancestors, and the third is for whatever the assembled Heathens agree upon.

Besides giving offerings to the gods, most Heathens leave small gifts for the domestic "hidden folk," like the wights who live in their yards. Many Heathens have a special bowl where they place their offerings. Some even have a small altar in their garden. Often, Heathens will make a small offering for their house wight whenever they are baking bread or brewing their own mead. They do this for good luck, and to shoo away the negative energy that can spoil their produce.

You also need to be respectful towards your house wight. You have to respect their space, which you can do simply by keeping your home clean. Always do your best to be in the good graces of your hidden folk.

Morality and Ethics

Although the name Heathen has always been associated with being uncivilized and without morals, that is the opposite of what real practitioners of the religion stand for. Heathens base their ethical and moral views on the actions by the characters in old Norse sagas. Their ethics focus mainly on the ideals of honor, hospitality, the virtue of hard work, courage, and integrity. They also strongly focus on family bonds.

The Heathen community expects members to keep their word all the time, most especially if they made a sworn oath. The main reason can be pointed to a strong individualist ethos that focuses mainly on personal responsibility. "We are our deeds" is a common motto used within the community. Most Heathenry practitioners reject the concept of sin. They believe that being guilted for your past actions is more destructive than it is useful.

Magic and Seership

It is common for members of the ancient Norse religion to partake in the practice of magic and divination. Every community has at least one person who practices the mystic arts. In modern Heathenry, many still believe and practice magic and divination. They are even actively reviving many practices used by the ancient Germanic cultures.

Practices that modern Heathens are actively reviving include the creation of runic talismans and the chanting of charms (galdor). Many are also rediscovering the Northern European divination practice called "seidh." "Oracular seidh" is an ancient ritual where a seer will answer questions or give advice to the participants.

Many modern Heathens also use runes to foretell the future. Foretelling might not be the right word here. One can use runes as oracles for advice. They give hints on how to find the answers to your questions, but it is you who will ultimately need to figure out the details. However, it is important for rune casters to have excellent intuition.

Runic divination is not fortunetelling per se. The runes will only give you a means of analyzing your path and determining the possible outcomes if you stay on the same course. Practitioners of rune divination do not particularly believe in predestination. According to them, your future is not set in stone. You can change your outcome by changing the present.

Chapter 2: The Divine Gift of Futhark

Now that you have had a quick introduction to Heathenry or, in other words, the modern Norse religion, it is time for you to learn more about the practice of divination and reading runes. Before you can learn rune divination, you need to understand how to read runes. The talismans you will be using later are all inscribed using a runic alphabet known as the Futhark, and this chapter will teach you all about this ancient writing system.

The Elder Futhark

In modern pop culture, the Norse/Germanic runes always seem to have mystical and mysterious properties. With that in mind, you can see their symbolism often being used in fantasy video games and tabletop games. Wiccan practitioners also use runes for their ceremonies and rituals, pretty much like modern Heathens use them.

The Germanic tribes of the Scandinavian isles had always used runes (well before Christianity came onto their shores). After most of the population were forced to convert to Christianity, runes and other old Heathen practices became known as pagan. It directly opposes Christianity. Hence, it was outlawed and almost wiped out of existence. The Christian colonizers could not eradicate the Germanic religion completely, and it only added intrigue and mystique to the runes.

The Runic alphabet, also known as the Futhark, is the system of writing used by the ancient Germanic tribes. The name came from the first six letters of the runes, namely F, U, TH, A, R, and K. It is pretty much the same way as when the alphabet came from alpha and beta, the first two letters of the Greek alphabet.

There are no clear explanations as to why the Futhark runes are arranged in such a peculiar way. Although no one knows the real answer, many experts believe that it is a form of the mnemonic function to make it easier to memorize the letters.

Mythical Origin of the Runes

Odin, the All-Father, has always been on a never-ending quest for more knowledge and wisdom. He is so relentless that he will sacrifice anything to get more knowledge, as evidenced by his one eye. He sacrificed his other eye in exchange for more wisdom, but that is another story.

Odin's discovery of the Germanic runes had him do many inconceivable things on himself. It is all thanks to his seemingly unquenchable thirst for understanding the myriad of mysteries in the cosmos. Also, it is a testament to his unshakeable will.

After Odin and his brothers defeated the giant Ymir, he created the realm of man, which he called Midgard. After finishing the creation of the Nine Realms, he hoped and wished to acquire more than enough wisdom so he could use it to watch over them.

It prompted him to send out Thought and Memory, two of his ravens, into various worlds throughout the day. The roles of his ravens include communicating with all creatures, whether or not they were dead or alive. They would come back at night to tell Odin about all the information they gathered during their exploration.

Odin continued with that setup until eventually, he tired of it. He felt unsatisfied with the specific manner through which he acquired wisdom and knowledge. This motivated him to look for and collect all his desired information by himself. This decision led to his seemingly endless pursuit of wisdom and knowledge.

Odin had a strong urge and desire to acquire knowledge, so he visited Mimir. He was the wisest man of the entire Aesir. Odin's wish was to acquire knowledge by drinking from Mimir's well. The reason was this powerful well held one root of Yggdrasil containing all information about the Nine Realms.

Odin relayed this intention to Mimir, but the latter informed him that to fulfill his intention, he had to sacrifice something. His sacrifice should be substantial and fitting for a god-like him. Odin was then asked to sacrifice one eye, and he never even once hesitated to do so. His hunger for knowledge made him agree to dig his left eye out and then give it to Mimir, but even after that incident, Odin still seemed insatiable with all his acquired knowledge.

He continued his exploration and quest until he learned about the magical runes and their secrets. He got intensely interested in them upon learning these mysterious symbols can give users complete control over the forces of nature, but he also knew the need to make a huge sacrifice to master the runes and understand them deeply. He knew that he might have to endure extreme suffering to where he would be on the brink of death.

He was prepared to do all that just to satisfy his need for knowledge. It was at this moment when he stabbed his side with a sword, then hung himself on the Yggdrasil's branches. He stayed that way for nine days without eating, drinking, or sleeping. He discovered the runes and their individual powers and mysteries successfully after getting close to death.

Odin also realized how useful the runes were when it came to doing even those seemingly impossible acts, like talking to the dead, healing those who are sick, predicting what will happen, and calling upon and calming storms. With this newly acquired knowledge, he had a strong desire to share it with the world. This promoted him to carve the first 18 runes in stone, wood, and bone. He even did the carving in the claws of a wolf and the beak of an eagle, too. After carving, he relayed all these items to everyone who lived in Midgard.

The Connection Between Wood and the Runes

The Futhark originated from the runes passed down by Odin, but the runes themselves retained their original powers. The ancient Norse Vikings and other Germanic tribes used runes whenever they wanted to talk to their fallen relatives or acquaintances. They also used them for protection and peace.

Aside from that, most also discovered that the runes were useful for divination and contacting beings who existed on the other planes of existence. They used different materials to draw the different runes on, including wood (most especially oak, beech, and pine), bones, shells, paper, or stone. Most believe that runes are more powerful if you create them yourself, instead of using the ones that other people made.

The most common material used for rune making is wood. It is mainly due to the wooden element's importance in Norse mythology. For instance, the Tree of Life, Yggdrasil, sustains the Nine Worlds from its branches. Most of the Norse artifacts with runes inscribed on them are made of wood.

Futhark in Britain

At around 400 to 500 AD, three Germanic tribes from Scandinavia, the Angles, Saxons, and the Jutes, invaded Britain. Along with their culture, they brought along the Futhark. As time went on, they modified the Futhark into the 33-letter "Futhorc" so it could accommodate the unique sounds that came with the Old English language, the language spoken by the Anglo-Saxons.

According to linguists, the "Futhorc" is evidence of the phonological change where the Old English long /a/ vowel evolved into the /o/ vowel sound. Initially, the Futhark/Futhorc writing system seemed to thrive in Britain. But it declined, and eventually, it almost disappeared with the spread of the Latin alphabet.

Futhorc went on the decline during the 9th century AD, and by the 10th century, missionaries converted all the Germanic tribes to Christianity. With the dissolution of their old way of life, their culture and the Futhark alphabet also slowly diminished.

Modern Believers

Even after a thousand years of finishing the Viking age, Thor and Odin, and the other gods and goddesses in the Norse religion, were still strong, with many people still believing in them. When Christianity was introduced, the old Nordic religion somehow declined or disappeared, but there is still a significant number of people who practice it. After Christianity was introduced, the Norse religion was practiced secretly. Some even practiced it while hiding under the cloak of Christianity.

Presently, you can still find many people from various parts of the world who believe in the Norse religion and magic. Around 500 to 1,000 people in Denmark still have a strong faith in this religion up to the present day. These people still worship the ancient gods.

Like what the Vikings did, most modern believers meet up openly. It is when they worship and praise the Gods they believe in and give offerings; among the rituals they do to honor their Gods are drinking a toast and eating a feast. For instance, some offer a toast to the Gods of fertility if their intentions include prosperity and an abundant harvest.

The toast could also be personal, such as when a woman wants to get pregnant or search for eternal love. For those struggling, they can praise Thor so they will become stronger. They can also invoke Odin to gain wisdom.

One thing to note about the modern belief and faith in the Norse Gods is that it does not serve as a direct succession of what the Vikings believed in. Generally, it focuses more on reinterpreting and reviving the old religion. The reason could be the limited written sources regarding this subject.

What Can Runes Be Used For?

Are you curious about the things that runes can help you with? As suggested by their historical origins, you can use them for many things, but unless you are a Norse god, you may not be able to use them to control the weather or talk to the dead just yet. However, you will still find them useful for several reasons and situations.

One specific situation where you can use runes is when you need guidance. - maybe a time when you find yourself in a rough patch in your life. This is called divination, which differs from fortune-telling, as it will not tell you a straight answer on how events will unfold. The runes will let you know about the different variables that may happen and what possible outcomes your actions can bring.

Runes will hint toward answers, but they will still let you work toward finding the details. With that in mind, have a keen intuition when using runes. Rune readers acknowledge that the future is not set in stone. This means you still have the power to make your own decisions that can change the outcomes.

If you do not like what the runes are saying about your future, you are free not to accept it and do the appropriate actions to prevent the divination from happening. You still have the chance to change your direction or go on a different path.

You can also use runes when you find yourself where you have limited information only before making a practical decision. It is always necessary to use your intuition to make sense of what they are telling you.

Again, casting runes differs from actual fortune-telling. The idea behind the way you use runes is that your conscious and subconscious minds focus on them whenever you ask them questions. When you cast them, your sub-conscious may have decided for you. The runes are just around to help make it clearer.

Some people believe that you can ask runes only about the issues that bother you specifically. Others believe that it is fine to ask specific questions. Regardless of what you ask, it is best to think of your query clearly. Remember that as you are casting your runes.

Also, remember that reading runes is not an exact science. You will not see a clear future outcome, nor will you get a clear answer to your question. Rune reading is more about using your intuition to look for possible outcomes.

Other Uses for Runes

Runes are not just tools used for divination but also powerful relics you can use for other purposes. Here are a couple of their other famous uses:

Jewelry

You can carve the rune symbols onto your jewelry. Here, you can use any precious metals you like. It is even possible for you to carve the runes onto gemstones if you want to. You may use your imagination as to what you inscribe runes onto. There is no wrong way of doing it if your intentions are in the right place. Don't worry about them backfiring. You can rest assured knowing that even if you use the runes improperly, they will only be ineffective instead of being dangerous.

Talismans

While inscribing runes onto jewelry is a passive method of using them (other people may view them as decorative designs), talismans are more obvious in their usage. These are large medallions with runic inscriptions. They also often have a large stone in the middle.

Heathen practitioners consider rune talismans as conscious and alive, which is why you can keep them permanently or make them in such a way you can release them once their intended purpose manifests. You can make that possible by burying the runes in the Earth, so they can return to nature.

Making the Best Runes

Historically, rune makers will use their blood or that of a sacrificial animal to pigment their runes, allegedly empowering them even more, but it is not really a requirement. As a matter of fact, you can use any kind of paint or ink you like, especially if you are the squeamish type who can't stand the sight of blood.

Consider timing when creating a rune. There, consider the phase of the moon at that moment. For instance, to create runes that represent the growth and accomplishment of goals, make them during a waxing moon. But the best time to create runes designed to eliminate or dispel is when there is a waning moon.

The most basic and easiest way to pick rune inscriptions is to write them horizontally. In the old days, rune inscriptions were done in odd numbers, but if you are not a fan of the traditional method, you can just choose any number you feel like using, but remember that sometimes, the "less is more" concept is more applicable. Rune inscriptions are among those times. Think of rune inscription as telling a story, so you are describing the outcome you want.

Some rune makers also enjoy chanting or singing the name of each rune every time they are creating them. You can also do that. The important thing is that you focus on charging the runes with your personal intentions while you are creating them.

How Does Rune Casting Work?

Again, casting runes differs from actual fortune-telling. The idea behind the way you use runes is that your conscious and subconscious minds focus on them whenever you ask the runes questions. When you cast them, your subconscious has decided for you. The runes just help to make it clearer.

What Sort of Runes Do You Need?

You can use different materials for runes. Among the most popular ones are stone, crystals, bones, metal, and wood. If you are just a beginner at reading runes and are still getting a feel for it, then using a basic/simple rune set will do. If you have been rune casting for years, you can get a special set for yourself.

If you feel like there is a certain attraction between you and a certain rune, like it is speaking out to you, then you should get it. When you purchase a set of runes, they usually come with a pamphlet explaining what each rune represents and the different options you can interpret them. It would be even better if you carved out your own set of runes. You can use crystals, animal bones, wood, or even metal for that purpose if you so wish.

Runes you make yourself have more power inside of them than pre-made ones. Regardless of the material or who made them, the thing that matters the most is what you do with them.

Chapter 3: The Fundamentals of Divination

Now that you have a bit of understanding about runes and their mystical and historical origins, you can learn how you can use them. Since using the mystical properties of runes, like weather control and talking to the dead, among many others, is still out of the hands of mere mortals, you can learn how to use them for divination. This process is also called rune casting.

What is Rune Casting?

Rune casting is a method of oracular divination, where the user lays out or casts the runes. It can either be in a specific pattern, or you can throw them randomly. It is a way for people to gain guidance on how to deal with their problems or face their situations. Basically, it gives a way for people to make sensible decisions.

Runes will not give you an exact answer to your inquiries. They cannot tell you when or how you will die, nor will it let you know who you will marry and when. You will not also receive any advice from runes. You can't expect them to tell you you should quit your job and become a professional gamer. They will not advise you to dump your cheating spouse and take the kids with you.

Runes will suggest the possible outcomes of your decision. Put simply, they will only give you hints. You will need to use your critical thinking skills and your intuition to figure out the best course of action for your situation.

Like with other kinds of divination methods, the answers from runic divination are not final. If you do not like what the runes are telling you, just change what you are doing and choose another path. You are still the master of your own destiny. The runes are just there as your guide.

How Easy is it to Interpret Runes?

Only a few people can pick up the art of rune divination on the first try. It will take time before you can call yourself a master of the art. Usually, when you buy a set of runes, it comes with an instructional pamphlet that shows how you can interpret them. You can consult many books and videos to learn as much as you can about runes, but they will most likely not be enough.

For many, learning how to interpret runes accurately will be a lifelong affair. Still, it can be an uplifting experience. You will also be delighted to know that eventually, reading them will get easier, especially if you practice.

If you have good intuition, it is much easier to figure out what the runes are potentially telling you. If you are unsure about the rune's message, don't worry, as it might not just relate to your current situation. Try to preserve as much of the information the runes are telling you. Write down the details of your divination, especially the ones whose details you are unsure of, and then find out if the details become more relevant later.

Even rune casters with many years of experience under their belt still admit that they do not understand the meanings of the runes they cast sometimes. Some even have to wait for weeks or months after the casting for answers to come to them.

The Importance of Meditating Before Rune Casting

Whether or not you are a beginner at rune casting or have been doing it for years, you have most likely tried different techniques to improve your rune reading accuracy. A few techniques you tried may have worked, while others did nothing. While you have learned quite a lot of new things, your rune reading prowess seems unchanged.

One method that seems to work for many rune casters – and most likely for you – is meditation. Why does meditation seem to work so well? The following reasons might explain it.

It Calms Your Mind, Letting You Think Clearly

Having a calm and relaxed mind will allow you to clear your thoughts and minimize any stress you are experiencing somehow. You need a clear mind because you will be trying to read the runes in a focused and deliberate manner. It is important to look at the runes you cast and try to make sense of them as best as you can. Note you are trying to figure out what is coming. Just doing these things is already difficult, and it gets even harder when you have a stressed-out mind.

For instance, after a stressful day at work or school, you come home, and a million thoughts are racing through your mind. You sit down and try to cast your runes, but the only thing going through your mind is the pile of paperwork you need to sift through at work or the looming test on Monday. Your mind is obviously not focused on the runes, which can lead to messing up your readings if there is anything there.

It Allows You to Access a Higher Level of Thought

What is a higher level of thought? It means you have complete focus on whatever task you have at hand. It is like you have tuned out the rest of the world and can only see and hear the task in front of you.

There are different levels of consciousness that the human mind can reach. The higher the level, the more awareness your mind has. You become more sensitive to the things that are happening around you and in your lower levels of consciousness. It is a great help for rune casters because a focused mind allows them to visualize things they could not visualize before.

It Gives You More Control Over Your Body and Mind

If you are like most rune casters, then you have most likely tried to find the best place in your home to do your readings, but you can't seem to find a setting completely quiet and free of distractions. You cannot completely escape distractions; the only thing you can do realistically is to train your mind so they will have no negative effects.

Meditation will help you train your mind so it can acclimatize itself to any situation that may happen. It will not make your mind completely blank nor numb to outside stimuli, but it will make you more mindful. Mindfulness means that your mind recognizes that there will be distractions wherever you go, but instead of letting these thoughts create a state of stress, you can acknowledge them and accept that they are there.

It promotes ease in willing your way through the distractions and focusing on your task, which, in this case, is rune casting. With mindfulness meditation, you can cast your runes even in the pouring rain. Any form of distraction will not bother you in the slightest.

How Meditation Can Help with Readings

Suppose you can place yourself into a higher level of thought due to meditation. There, you will immediately discover that, even if you are not actively meditating, your senses are still more aware than ever. Every time you open your senses to the everyday world, you exercise and continuously train your mind to see things differently. You will have other perspectives where you can base your decisions.

Because you are more in tune with your surroundings, you can easily pick up the smaller details you may have otherwise missed, helping you make sense of the runes better. For instance, when you sit down with a person for a rune reading, you can get a grasp of his or her personality. You can read other people better so you can give them a more accurate interpretation of the runes.

Here is a sample scenario. You have a friend who is going for a job interview next week, and he wants to know if he will get the job. Being his friend, you already know that he is the kind of person who will tense up during an interview but is also very qualified.

You also know the job your friend is interviewing for involves dealing with other people, so it is important for him to work on his people skills. In that case, you may cast your runes. Perhaps Uruz is the most important. Uruz is a rune for power –but it is one out of people's control. It can also mean that success is nearby.

Typically, you can tell your friend that success is near, but it comes with a power he has no control over. Also, you are not sure when this power will come. If you meditate before the reading and are in a more mindful state, you can sense your friend's attitude about the job. If you feel that your friend is in control, it is highly likely that the power without control comes with the job.

Preparing for Rune Casting

Do you think that you are already ready to cast runes? If you are, then know there are still a couple more things you need to do to bring yourself to the right headspace. Rune castings and readings require you to be comfortable and prepared before you start.

As a disclaimer, these tips are not requirements for a rune reading. The only thing you need will be a set of runes. You know yourself better than anyone else, so you are the only one who can say what makes you comfortable before doing a reading.

However, here are a few suggestions depending on certain key factors:

Time of Day

Some rune casters believe that castings should be done only during the day. It should always be outside with the sun shining brightly. But some say that the best time is just before midnight. It is the time when the veil separating this world and the other world is at its thinnest. It means it is easier to communicate with the spirits.

Some also say there is a way to calculate which time is best to do a reading, depending on the questions you will be asking. The time you do the reading will depend on your preferences. There is no evidence that proves one way is better than the others. The better thing to do is to do your castings during different times of the day and see which times suit you best.

Weather

The weather plays a huge role when rune casting and reading. It was mentioned earlier that some casters prefer sunny days rather than overcast or rainy days. The main reason is that the weather can influence a person's mood. For instance, most people feel inexplicably sad when the sky is grey or when it is raining, and they feel more positive when the sun is shining. Some people also feel more comfortable when it is overcast outside or raining. The most important thing here is to schedule your casting during a time when the weather and your mood are at their best.

Surroundings

Your surroundings also play a huge part when you are rune casting. The reason could be each location has its own unique energy field. For instance, you may not want to cast somewhere with plenty of power lines or cellular towers as the energy they give off may interfere with your own.

Also, consider the kind of people who are around you. It is best to avoid those who are skeptical or do not believe in the power of the runes outright. If you surround yourself with highly skeptical people, they will influence your own feelings about the runes. You may even doubt yourself, thus resulting in a poor and inaccurate reading.

Casting Set-Up

If you are rune casting outdoors, then the setup you have to go for should be simple and basic. You just need to face the sun, lay out your casting cloth (if you will be using one), place your pillow, and then sit on it. Across from you, place your mearmots and a piece of paper that contains the question you wish to ask the runes (optional).

Put your hand inside the rune pouch and mix up the runes. Gather the number of runes you need depending on the casting type, then toss them onto the casting cloth or right in front of you.

If you fancy casting indoors, then you can use a couple of setups. First, find a space that is big enough so you can lay out your casting cloth with nothing in its way. The cloth should also be flat and not bunched up.

If possible, sit facing east or wherever the sun's position is at the time. If you are casting at night, set your layout so you face the moon. If these setups are impossible in your home, just lay the cloth so nothing obstructs it – that will be fine.

A Quick Overview of the Casting Procedure

Now, onto casting the runes. Some magical traditions do the process by casting or tossing the runes onto a white cloth. The cloth provides a clear background for reading the runes and a magical boundary extremely useful during the casting process.

Some casters do it directly on the ground. As the one who will be doing the casting, you have the freedom to pick the method you want. Once the casting session ends, get a small box or pouch where you can store them.

You can cast runes using any of the many methods available. Each one of them is as valid as the next. There are a couple of layouts that are currently popular with modern rune casters.

Like other divination methods, rune casting basically addresses one particular issue and lets you look for the things that could influence it from your past and present. For instance, you may want to do a 3-rune cast by pulling three one at a time from the pouch. You can then place them side-by-side on a white cloth.

The first rune you pulled out represents the general overview of your situation. The second one is for the challenges and obstacles in your way, while the last one gives you the potential paths you can take in response.

Here is how a basic rune casting session would usually start:

- Lay out your runes on the cloth, all facing up to make sure that the set is complete. After that, you can put them back inside the pouch.

- Place your hand inside the pouch and mix them up as best as you can. While doing so, concentrate on your question.

- Pick up a couple of runes that will depend on the casting method you chose and toss them onto the cloth.

- Use the runes that landed face up to do your reading. If you do not have enough runes facing upward to do your reading, you can choose to re-cast and start over again, re-cast the runes that landed face-down or leave the spaces in the spread blank.

How to Pick the Runes from the Casting Cloth

Once the runes are on the casting cloth, the next thing that may cross your mind is how to figure out which ones to pick up. Fortunately, there are a couple of ways to do so. The first involves picking a spot on the cloth before you cast them. Then pick up the rune closest to it for the first spot on the spread. After that, pick the one closest next. Continue doing so until all the spaces in your spread are full.

Another way is to imagine a line running down the center of the casting cloth and then pick up the face-up rune that lands closest to it first. If two runes are somewhat the same distance from the line, pick the one closest to you first. The spots in your spread are full; the next step is to read them and figure out their meanings.

Chapter 4: The Runemaster's Tools

Now that you have the basic gist of rune casting and reading, it is time for you to prepare your own tools for divination. The primary tools that all rune casters need to have are the runes themselves. There, you can choose to either make the runes on your own or buy them.

Making Your Own Runes

If you are just learning about runes, making your own set is a good way for you to memorize each runic symbol. Painting or carving the symbols onto your desired media can serve as a sort of meditation, which is also helpful in infusing more of your energy into your runes.

Depending on how skilled you are with your hands and your level of adeptness at crafts, and the materials you have to work with, making your own rune sets can be a good outlet for your creativity. If you create your own Elder Futhark runes, then you will need 24 similar-sized objects for your rune tiles (25 if you will be including a wyrd rune).

You can usually find the perfect materials in your local craft store. To go through it in the same way as the ancient Nords did, you can find the materials you will need right in your backyard.

The great thing about buying from the craft store is that you can easily get uniformly shaped tiles, as opposed to going to your local stream and spending hours searching for pebbles roughly the same size and shape.

Searching through nature for the materials for your runes makes the process more spiritual. The runes you make will also be highly personal and unique. Making your own runes has these pros and cons:

Pros

• It allows you to build a more personal connection with your runes.

• It gives you the chance to exercise your creativity since you will be the one to create a unique set of runes.

• More budget-friendly compared to buying them

Cons

• Unless you are skilled and have the right materials and equipment, you might not get runes that are as beautiful as the commercially available ones.

Buying Commercially Available Runes

Meanwhile, a lot of specialty shops and websites nowadays offer pre-made rune sets. You can just purchase them if you do not want to deal with the hassle of making one on your own. Pre-made ones are often constructed helped by techniques and materials hard to replicate by anyone. It may even be more challenging to replicate them if you are not the crafty type.

You can get runes that are laser-engraved, especially if you want the inscriptions to be permanent. You can also find those with beautiful inlays. If you do not have the necessary tools, equipment, and skills to do such meticulously crafted items, it is better to invest your money in pre-made ones. It is especially true if you feel that a certain rune set is calling out to you.

Usually, commercially available sets contain the twenty-four runes popularized by the Futhark. Most of these runes also feature a wyrd or blank rune, which serves as a wild card. As it is pre-made, you can expect each one also to have its own decorative box or drawstring pouch. Most also contain instructions so users will not have a hard time familiarizing themselves with the runes and the basics of using them.

Note, though, that just because these extra items come with the runes, you are under no obligation to use them and the specific instructions about their usage. Rune reading techniques vary, and no two casters use the same exact method of going about it.

Pros

• Offers several options

• Several unique and beautifully made runes are available for sale – Some are so unique that you simply cannot replicate them.

• Always uniform in size and design

Cons

• It will be challenging to build a strong spiritual bond with your runes since you just bought them.

Materials

Some materials that make great runes include wood nickels, sawn-off slices from a tree branch, kiln-fired clay tiles, or glass aquarium rocks. Basically, anything that is small and uniform in size will work well.

Now, also consider the durability of the material. Some people used flat rocks they got from riverbeds only to discover later that they were fragile sedimentary rocks that tend to chip and disintegrate easily. Uncured wood will crack and split along the grain.

Painted symbols on a smooth surface would usually chip off when the runes scrape against each other in the pouch. It will take trial-and-error before you can find a material that will be durable enough to last at least a year or two of constant rune readings.

The following are suggestions on the kind of material that you can use to make your rune set.

Bone - You can make runes out of animal bones cleaned and left out in the sun to bleach and dry. You can also use these bones if you are a collector of these materials. With that, you will have ready materials for making the runes, specifically the skeletal remains of animals.

When planning to use animal bones, a wise tip is to look for the thickest and densest ones. The reason is that thick and dense bones are highly recommended for rune-making. Upon research, you may also realize how easy it will be to work on a rune if you use femurs.

If you are not a collector and you are just planning to purchase the bones for the runes, then be prepared to look for the ones from water buffaloes, as these are ideal. The reason is that the commercially available ones are made from such animals. These bones are also known for being by-products of dairy and meat farming in Asia.

Antlers – The deer antlers' cross-sections are also great materials for rune-making. The neat thing is that you need not hunt deer just to get their antlers. Early winter is when the rutting season ends, and male deer will shed their antlers. You will usually find the discarded antlers near the base of the trees in the woods inhabited by the deer.

To connect with the Stag energy, then deer antlers are the best choice for making your runes. Keep them away from your dog, as deer antler runes look a lot like dog kibble!

Wood - You can use any kind of wood you want for making your rune set. You can stick to the types that, according to folklore, have magical properties, like Ash, Elder, and Oak. You are still free to pick any wood with a personal significance, like the branches of the tree in your backyard you planted when you were young.

If you are using fresh woods from trees, then make sure to dry them thoroughly first to prevent them from splitting. You need not go through this step if you will be buying your wood commercially since those have been kiln-dried already.

Stone - Heathenry practitioners say that any rune made of stone is already a modern invention. Some even believe that the only materials designed for rune-making are bones and wood. It is just a misconception as you can work on any material you can think of. If you can inscribe your runes, then it is all good, so the stone is also a great idea.

One probable reason wood and bone were used back in the day is that they were readily available and relatively easy to carve compared to stones. You can use precious or semi-precious gems or just ordinary pebbles to make your runes. It does not necessarily need to be expensive. Gemstone runes are undoubtedly beautiful, and they have a nice heft to them, making them nice to cast.

You can also choose gemstones known for having magical properties to bolster the powers of the runes even further. For instance, you can make them out of jasper for courage and hematite for protection.

Ceramic - You can also find runes made from clay, either air-dried, oven-baked, or fired in a kiln. Of the three, the kiln-fired tiles are the most durable. Ceramic tiles are the most popular with DIY casters because they are the easiest to paint or carve.

Aside from that, this material seems to connect well with the Earth element. You can buy pre-made ceramic tiles you can paint or engrave. You can use broken floor tiles or pots. Just re-shape them to your preference.

Glass and Pewter - Glass and pewter runes are somewhat specialty items, making them hard to come by. The trouble with using glass beads and pewter beads is that they can be hard to paint, as their surfaces are too smooth for the paint to stay onto them properly.

The only way to inscribe runes on them is by etching (sandblasting or acid etching) or by carving. Both methods require special equipment, skill, and steady hands. Even though these materials are difficult to work with, the results will be more than worth the extra effort.

Are there certain materials you should not make into runes? The answer is there is no limit as to what you can use. The important thing about making runes you have to know is that you have to do it with the utmost respect. Odin hung half-dead on Yggdrasil for nine days and nights just to gain the knowledge of the runes.

With that in mind, it would seem disrespectful just to carve the symbol onto cheap Styrofoam and call it a rune. The least you can do is put effort into making your runes presentable and choosing the best materials for your intended purpose.

Size and Shape

Now that you have a handle on the specific materials you can use, it is time to think about the size and shape of the runes you will be making. Most runes, especially the ones in the form of gemstones, are usually around half an inch in diameter, which is too small for practical rune readers.

If you want your runes to be easy to read and feel comfortable in your hands, then you should get bigger ones or make them a bit bigger, like ¾-inch to 1-inch in diameter. This size is also beneficial if you will mostly do readings for others.

Runes come in different sizes and shapes, even when they are in the same set. If you plan to use the blind draw method of rune casting often, then it is important for your runes to have roughly the same size and shapes. This can help prevent making biased draws.

Should your runes be flat, round, symmetrical, or asymmetrical? Rounded runes feel good in the hands when drawing from a pouch, but they have the tendency to roll around too much when you cast them onto the casting cloth. If you are thinking of setting lines or grids with your runes, go with tiles or at least flat circular stones.

Another thing you must consider is whether you intend to read reversed runes. Reversals give different meanings to runes that landed face-down or upside-down. It's hard to tell if a rounded rune is lying face down or on its side. Certain runes also look the same upside-down and right-side-up. If you are dealing with such issues, it would be best for you to use asymmetrical runes and memorize the right orientation of each.

Inscribing the Runes

You can inscribe the Futhark letters onto your medium of choice. Take note, though, that some are more difficult than the rest. Nevertheless, they will still produce beautiful and lasting designs.

Here are just a few of the different ways to inscribe the runes:

Paints/Ink

Most DIY rune casters like to use paints or ink to mark their runes. It is essential to choose the right pigment based on the material you will be using. For instance, if you will be using stones, use acrylic paint as it is the only type that can adhere to stone surfaces.

You can also use different ink markers to write the runes onto the stones. It is the easiest and quickest method for making runes, but it also seems to have the lowest rank as to their durability. Speaking of durability, you will need to put a layer or two of clear varnish to protect the writing and make them last.

Carving

If you want something permanent, rather than simply painting or writing the runes on the surface, then be prepared to carve or engrave the Futhark letters into the tiles. Granted, these methods will need more skill, and if you are inexperienced, you may even cut your hands if you are not careful. Even if they don't come out perfectly, they will still look much better compared to painted runes. Aside from that, you can be assured that it will last a lot longer.

Wood-Burning

This method involves a soldering iron or a true wood-burning wand. It requires the use of a small electronic heating element over the surface of the wood, leaving a burnt, charred line on the surface. The charred line will not be easy to erase unless you sand off a lot of material from the surface of the wood.

You can also use this technique on bone tiles, but you must do it in a well-ventilated area because it may create noxious fumes.

Chapter 5: Rune Preparation: From Cleansing to Empowering

Do you want your runes to work as efficiently as they did when you first made and used them? Then you need to take good care of them, but unlike taking care of other kinds of accessories, maintaining runes does not just entail cleaning them the orthodox way. It entails cleansing and charging them, and you will be learning more about these tasks in this chapter.

Note that runes can be powerful tools, especially when you treat them with care and respect. You will need to cleanse and empower them, especially if they are still new or many people have already touched them.

One thing to remember is that runes are private and personal items, and their owners should be the only ones who keep and see them. You can place them on your desk or in your workspace. It could also be somewhere near your bed.

By keeping them close, you are letting them tune into your personal energy, leading to clearer and more concise rune readings. If you are using them often for reading other people, you will need to cleanse them more often.

Cleansing

There are many ways for you to cleanse your runes. You can choose whatever takes your fancy, but the most important thing is you do it often and regularly. Cleansing is even more important between uses or when you accidentally surround them with another person's energy for too long.

Here are ways to cleanse your runes so they can work properly once again:

- Laying them out at night, or early in the morning, and leaving them out for at least 24 hours.

- Smudging - This method involves passing them through the smoke of smoldering herbs that contain purifying properties primarily designed to cleanse them. If you live somewhere where even a small fire can make your neighbors panic, you can substitute the herbs for a white candle.

- Using natural flowing water, you can also cleanse them using natural flowing water, like a creek or a nearby stream. Never use tap water for cleansing as it has gone through numerous treatment processes, but if you have a bit of rainwater saved in a container in your home, you can use that instead.

Empowering

You can empower your runes simply by keeping them close. You can do so by always carrying them in your pocket or bag. Another way to do it is to keep them within your personal space. That way, they can tune themselves to your personal energy.

Here are other tips you can use:

- Place them outside so the sun can bless them - Just leave the runes outside at the crack of dawn, then bring them back into your home just before dusk.

- Bury your rune set into the soil - You can either bury them in one single pile or put them in a pouch and then bury them. You can dig them up after at least a week has passed.

On the other hand, you can also perform a small but intricate cleansing ceremony. First, cast a circle to chase away any negative energy, then cleanse the space and yourself using the smoke from a smoldering pile of sage. Lay down your casting cloth in the middle of the circle and your runes for cleansing.

Bless the runes with the elements. In this part, you can choose whatever has meaning for you. For instance, for the earth element, sprinkle rock salt. Pass them through the smoke of the sage for the air element. Sprinkle rainwater over them for the water element.

Finally, pass them through the flame of a lit red candle for the fire element. After you finish with the elements, hold each rune tightly in your right hand to imbue each with your spirit.

If you usually use the runes to guide others, it is best to cleanse them before and after every use. Also, it is advisable to re-empower your runes every full moon.

The Proper Way to Store Your Runes

You can store your rune set in a bag, preferably made of a natural material. You also may use any pouch you fancy. You can place them in a wooden box.

Most rune casters use casting cloths, and it is common to find them paired with a particular rune set. If you will be using a casting cloth, it is best to stay consistent with its color and/or material when switching cloths. Doing so will let the runes get in tune with the casting cloth and vice versa.

Like the runes themselves, you should also regularly cleanse the item where you store them because it is essentially their home.

Empowering Yourself

When you continually work with your runes, you will gradually learn more about nature's power. You will understand your place in the universe, allowing you to experience growth in all aspects.

Nature teaches you about maintaining balance and being in harmony. By regularly communing with nature and the elements within, you cannot help but feel enlightened. You feel empowered, as well. Do it regularly, and you will find a true connection with the Universe.

Aside from communing with nature, you can also wear runic symbols on your person to empower yourself. Runes give out powerful vibrations that can serve as protection against harm. They will attract their specific qualities toward your life. Wearing a rune around your neck, like a talisman, will subject your entire being to it and all its related influences.

How to Consecrate Runes

If you just bought or made a new set of runes, or have been using it for a while already, then you should consecrate it first before using it again. Aside from re-energizing your rune set, it will also make your readings more uniform and accurate.

Consecration means to make something holy. When you consecrate your runes, you are turning them from regular stones or tiles into sacred tools for divination.

The great thing about runes is that you can re-consecrate them infinitely. If you realize that your readings have become less clear or accurate as of late, then you will need to consecrate them as soon as you can. You also have to do the consecration if you have not used your runes for a long time and they do not work like they used to anymore.

One thing to remember about consecrating runes is that you are not just purifying and preparing them for use but also creating a spiritual link between them and you. It is the reason you need not be a psychic to use runes. The runes themselves will serve as the bridge between you and the divine.

If you know how to read the runic symbols, you become a sort of interpreter to the divine. You can use them to gain guidance from the other realms in the universe. When you cast and read them, you will discover that they tell a sort of story. You will discover patterns and trends you can use to figure out your next best course of action.

By consecrating your rune set and yourself in the process, you are helping yourself to open up to the messages/story hidden in the runes. It is true whether or not you use them for yourself or if you like to give readings to other people.

Even though you do not have to be a psychic to read runes, your perception will increase. It will increase so that you will know the answers even before you cast your runes. Every time it happens, keep track of everything that pops into your head regarding the reading, then check later if they confirm any of your earlier thoughts.

Now, on to the actual consecration process. Just like cleansing, there is no one method of consecrating runes. If you follow the basic requirements, then you will be fine.

First, you will need purifying smoke. Most heathenry practitioners use sage as its smoke has purifying qualities. Some people do not like sage as the smell of its smoke can be overpowering. If so for you, then you can use incense. For consecration, you cannot go wrong by choosing traditional frankincense and myrrh.

But if you are not a fan of fragrances, you can use a white candle instead. The warm light given off by the candle can also serve as a catalyst. You can choose whatever method works best for you.

Here are the basic steps for the basic consecration ceremony:

- Light the bundle of sage/incense and allow the smoke to flow over you and purify yourself and the container of your runes.

- Hold your runes using the non-dominant hand. Hold it over the sage/incense smoke or over the flame of the white candle. It should be just high enough over it that you feel no pain.

- Seek your deity's aid for protection and protect your runes from all, save for the highest forms of energy.

- Look at each run and connect with them one by one. Imagine your energy going into each and becoming one with it. Now, with your non-dominant hand, hold them all again and place them over the smoke.

Ask your chosen deity to consecrate them so you can use them to help yourself and others.

After cleansing and consecrating your set, you can use it immediately. When not in use, store them in a soft pouch or a lined box so they remain sacred and safe.

Chapter 6: Aettir: The Mother, the Warrior, and the King

According to many academic and occult books that focus on runes, the Elder Futhark consists of three aettir (aett for its singular form). Aettir's existence did not get a lot of attention even after the runes regained their fame, though, since the Enochian alphabet lacks its similar division.

The only things that form part of the Enochian alphabet's internal structure are numerology and alphabetic order. You can also see these two divisions in the Hebrew alphabet with an additional division between single, mother, and double letters. The only time when the use of aettir was mentioned was when they served as the basis of ciphers, like tents and twig runes.

Despite that, it is still important to understand aettir as it relates to the Norse magic and rune creation. The reason is that it plays a huge role, serving as the basis for numerology in runes, which is already a complex subject on its own. It serves as a system with a few implications regarding the use of runes. Aside from implying an initiatory structure, the aettir also reflects the ancient Aryan tribal society's division consisting of the nurturer (mother), the warrior, and the king (priest).

The Three Divisions

As mentioned earlier, the Aettir structures the runes in a way they have three divisions. Each division or group, called an Aett, has exactly eight runes. Each aett has the name of a God matching the group's or family's runes. Aside from that, all the Aettir concealed specific teachings individually. Also, you will notice each rune composing a similar aett to be connected with each other.

Frey – The Mother

Frey is the first group or family, which symbolizes fertility. It is the reason it is also classified as the Mother. It serves as the vital force together with the way it is demonstrated inside the human body. It is also about awakening your consciousness. As the first Aett, the Frey signifies the first few steps you have to take for your enlightened future. This means it is something you should track to reach your ultimate goal.

Heimdall – The Warrior

The God, Heimdall, leads this second division. He is viewed as the God of silence sometimes, which others also perceive as priestly meditation. In essence, though, Heimdall can be considered a warrior. He is a watchful warrior, capable of facing struggles and dealing with overwhelming odds. It is in his watchfulness wherein he shows endless courage.

Tyr – The King

This group, which can also be viewed as the King, shows people's relationship with the divine forces. It also encompasses the roles they play in fate. This aett also refers to the human condition. It symbolizes social aspects and men and women's spiritual transformation.

You will get to know more about these three divisions (Aettir) in this book's succeeding chapters.

What Does the Elder Futhark Runes Represent?

The three mentioned divisions come with their own set of runes (8 for each aett, specifically). Each aett that forms part of each division has complementary functions. Each also boasts of its own unique character. A total of 24 elder Futhark runes, each one has these characters:

- Symbol portrayed by the rune and what it means

- Rune's exact name – This also signifies the word's meaning and its value in the form of a letter.

- Energy composing the rune – This also encompasses the specific reason why those who practice the rune view it as a living symbol.

The energy connected to each rune is not still and static. It is in motion all the time. It changes and even evolves into other forms. By tradition, the Norse made use of runes to convey information from one generation to another. With that, it is no longer surprising to see these runes informing anyone interested in the cosmos legend and how the energies existed.

By understanding all these energies on a deeper level, you also get to understand the specific reasons they affect your life and how. Also, remember that each rune represents the whole of each cosmic energy that composes all the aettir. With that, it is possible for you to view these energies as treasure maps – those capable of showing you a clear path you can follow to achieve divinity.

Once you gain a full understanding of the runes and the manner through which you can use them, it will indicate that you are following Odin's footsteps. You follow his quest and hunger for knowledge as he seems to continue searching for wisdom even after becoming a god.

Contradictions in Runes

When trying to gather information about all the runes to master them, you will most likely realize that each rune comes with polarities. For instance, Fehu and Uruz, the first two runes composing Frey, the first aett, are classic examples there are contradictions. The reason is that while Fehu symbolizes fire, Uruz is a symbol of ice.

You can also expect to see the same contradictions within just one rune. Fehu, for example, signifies mobile wealth, knowledge, great riches, and the capacity to succeed in a lot of things. Fehu also feeds your jealousy, greed, and inability to achieve your personal goals now and then.

With these contradictions around, it is crucial to gain a full comprehension of the specific manner through which the polarities work. This is important, especially if your goal is to make the runes work favorably for you despite the contradictions you detected. With your knowledge and understanding, you can take full advantage of the runes, especially for enriching your life and that of others.

What to Expect from the Three Aettir?

Basically, the first aett is a symbol of creation. The second one is all about the human element, while the third one is all about achieving divinity. It is at this exact point where you can expect to see the energies getting unified. The good thing about each aettir is that it aims to end favorably. Among those that you can expect from each aettir in the end ae:

- Wunjo, ushering practitioners to the Golden Age
- Sowilo, which signifies the sun

- Othala, symbolizing the leap you have taken from a regular plane to the next level. This will prompt the start of the circular process again.

Do you remember the time when Odin was nearly at death while he was still hanging from the branches of Yggdrasil? It was also the time when he pushed himself deliberately to move from one rune and aett to the next. This was the move he took to acquire all sacred knowledge and wisdom in each one.

It is also important to know all aetts have individual sections, outlining and tackling every bit of information related to each rune. This section informs you about the numerous methods you can use to take full advantage of each rune, especially in achieving your goals.

Here, you will discover limitless energy patterns that can greatly influence your personality and your present activities, and your future, especially if you stick to your present path. Note that each of your actions has waves of energy. Each action develops ripples and stimulates certain reactions and responses that help in balancing them.

Generally, maintaining the right balance between each rune's contradictions is important. Like Odin's past actions, it is possible for you to go back to the divine, the specific aspect where you came from once you work with the energies of the runes and comprehend their wisdom completely. It is what will help you fulfill the runes' circle.

After completing one aett, you will be led to a new one with a higher level of understanding, and this cycle will continue endlessly. There is never an end in the quest for more knowledge. There is always room for new experiences and new levels of understanding.

If you think that you already understood Othala, which is the last letter of the Futhark, then you can study what Fehu can do for your daily life. It means that a new cycle of learning has begun.

The three aetts represent the stages in a journey wherein you, the traveler, need to deal with the mundane and the spiritual, best the obstacles that come your way, learn how to read and understand important information, and take time to rest and refocus before you start once again. Such is the way of the runes.

Chapter 7: Freya's Aett

This chapter will teach you all about the first aett of the Futhark, which is Freya's aett. For each rune, you will get an explanation on how to pronounce them, their meaning, how to interpret them during divination, and other pertinent information.

When learning the runic alphabet, remember that every rune can have multiple meanings. You will need to use your intuition to figure out which meaning fits into your rune reading circumstances. You need to know all the meanings, so you can recall them easily whenever you are doing a reading for yourself or someone else.

The first of the three Aettir belongs to Freya, who is the Norse goddess of love, beauty, and fertility. This aett handles all aspects of love, happiness, pleasure, physical presence, and human emotions. Freya's aett is also symbolic of new beginnings, creation, and growth.

Here are the first eight runes included in Freya's Aett to start you learning how to read the runes.

Fehu

Sound: "f"

Meaning: Cattle, Wealth, Gold

Fehu is the rune that symbolizes new beginnings and the start of a new journey. It also became the first letter in the Futhark. Fehu's definition of cattle symbolizes wealth and material possessions. If you have cattle, then it means you are wealthy. Material wealth also includes money in all its forms. It is not just about physically owning the currency.

Because Fehu is the first of the letters in the runic alphabet, it also represents new and fresh beginnings. Another meaning you can derive from the Fehu rune is good luck, strength, and hope.

This rune also symbolizes the Cosmic Fire streaming towards the Cosmic Ice. With that, it is no longer surprising why it can help you set things in motion. Fehu symbolizes the ring of fire you need to go through to discover new things or seek mysteries.

The thing about new beginnings is that they can be quite scary. Usually, such beginnings will require you to jump blindly into unknown territory. There, you can use Fehu to help you take that all-important first step.

In the later runic poems, Fehu is said to connect with the mystery of wealth. Remember that just using this rune or any other will not make you rich automatically. In the poems, the Fehu rune says that you need to circulate your wealth and your skills. You also have to deal them out freely to attract more wealth your way. Simply put, you need to give wealth to gain it.

To use the rune Fehu, you can work them into sigils for good luck, wealth, and abundance. It is also useful in spells that aim to reach similar goals. You can inscribe the symbol of Fehu in an amulet to encourage wealth and strength to come to you.

Uruz

Sound: "oo" (letter "u")

Meaning: Auroch, an extinct species of Northern European wild cattle

Uruz mainly symbolizes strength and vitality. Like the wild oxen this rune represents, Uruz will impart strength (physical and mental) and vitality upon the caster.

You can look at Uruz as the wild and more primal counterpart of Fehu, symbolized by domesticated oxen. When they roamed the European plains, the Aurochs were among the fastest and strongest of all the beasts in the land. It represents brute strength and primal power that allows it to resist getting tamed. Uruz is also symbolic of freedom. Aside from that, it is the creative force that drives new beginnings.

Uruz represents man's primal instinct and power. It also symbolizes the success you can only receive through hard work. Uruz is symbolic of the clash between two opposing forces of Fire and Ice. You can use this rune to transfigure living things and impart healing energy. It can also promote faster and more effective healing to those who are ill. Aside from that, you can use it on any task or situation that requires any form of strength.

The shape of this rune came from the horns of the majestic and strong aurochs. In legends and real life, the oxen are mighty, and sometimes, they are even holy. Oxen and cows provide sustenance. In some myths, they also helped in creating the cosmos. It is the reason aurochs, and in connection with Uruz, can be associated with raw strength and vitality.

If you place the rune Uruz on objects, you can use it to bolster defensive magic. Many people hang a horseshoe over the front door of houses for protection and good luck. The main reason behind it is that it looks like the rune Uruz.

You can use the rune Uruz during those times when you find the need to bolster or increase your strength. One scenario is getting into new endeavors or whenever you need to increase your creativity.

Thurisaz

Sound: "th" (corresponds to the sound rather than the letters)

Meaning/s: This rune represents the god, Thor, as he is the protector of the Aesir. It can also represent the giants and their resilience.

Heathenry practitioners believe this rune is symbolic of the human will and resistance against physical and mental assault. With that in mind, Thurisaz became one of the most popular runes among those who practice heathenry.

According to experts, Thurisaz's definition is about passive defense or protection against danger and negative energies. Think of how thorns protect the rose bush. The rose bush need not do anything to prevent animals and people from getting too close. The thorns will provide more than enough protection.

Thurisaz can also mean transformation or the process of discarding what no longer works for you so you can make room for other positive things that may come your way. It is a symbol of abrupt changes or scenarios wherein you need to make an important choice.

Thurisaz is Thor's rune, which is why it represents force and will. The energy of this rune is a reactive force. It symbolizes the way of pure action and impenetrable will. It is the action that one plans for, which is like an impulsive shield that goes up instantly to protect your mind from attacks. You can use it to protect yourself against mental invasions, including dangerous curses.

Thurisaz is also purported to represent the poisoned needle that supposedly placed Sleeping Beauty under an eternal sleep. You can use Thurisaz to cause sleep or otherwise awaken someone from a mystical slumber.

As you can probably tell by now, you can inscribe this rune into sigils and amulets that provide protection. Aside from protection, you can consult it for guidance when making important and somewhat life-changing decisions.

Ansuz

ᚨ

Sound: "ah" (a)

Meaning: This rune symbolizes the divine, specifically the Aesir and other deities.

Practitioners of heathenry believe that Ansuz is the rune of the mind and awareness. It is also called the rune of Odin. It represents everything about communication and wisdom. Aside from that, it symbolizes basically anything that concerns words. Whether you are seeking advice, heeding help in studying for upcoming tests (particularly verbal ones), and connecting with your inner voice, you will discover that they all, and probably more, fall under the rune Ansuz.

If you are looking into strengthening other runes, Ansuz is the one you need. You can also use it to limit runes' powers. It is also the one associated with tools used for thought and memory.

This rune has a connection with inspiration and, by association, with the arts. It is the reason you can usually find the rune inscribed on or watermarked onto sketchbooks, desks, parchments, quills, and anything related to writing and drawing.

Regarding the manner through which you can use this rune, one scenario is when you need help with communicating with others. You will also find it useful in effective decision-making and in ensuring that you can easily make divination.

Raido

Sound: "r"

Meaning: Raido represents the journey of a ride, particularly a cart. It is also called the rune of order and correctness.

Raido symbolizes any kind of journey, travel in general, or even a means of transportation/vehicle. The type of journey does not matter. Whether you are physically transporting yourself from one place to another or trying to experience a spiritual or emotional journey, the rune Raido symbolizes them all.

Consulting this rune will show you the different options you can take to reach your destinations. You can also consult it when you need advice on what you need to do to accomplish the goals you set for yourself. Aside from that, this rune can signify your need to decide on something important and otherwise.

Raido also represents good counsel, one that will lead you to the right path. You can find this right path when you think rationally, consider your situation, and weigh your possible courses of action depending on both reason and your tradition. With that, many members of royalty and elected public officials would often wear clothes inscribed with this rune.

Heathenry practitioners also use Raido in rituals to ensure there will be no mistakes made during the event. You may also want to inscribe the rune on the floor where you will often do your readings as it will minimize, if not eliminate, your chances of making mistakes.

Moreover, Raido is valuable for maintaining your rhythm. If you are a musician or a performer where rhythm is imperative, this rune can help you keep up with the beat.

You can incorporate it on amulets or a charm to protect you during your journeys. It can help you make important decisions that will let you move your life in the right direction.

Kenaz

Sound: "k"

Meaning: Kenaz represents the torch, more specifically, the light that emanates from it.

When you feel troubled because you believe that nothing is going right and you want to change the course of your fate, Kenaz can help you by illuminating the path ahead of you. With its illumination, you can see where you need to go. According to practitioners, Kenaz is the rune responsible for all aspects and forms of creativity.

Every time a good idea pops into your head, it is like a light bulb is turned on just to clear your mind of everything. Kenaz is responsible for that sudden burst of inspiration you just had. The reason is this rune is all about clarity, enlightenment, discovery, and knowledge.

You can also connect this rune to the element of fire as it can illuminate the path in front of you. In addition, it can destroy the obstacles on your path or clear the way so you will see even more options to take on your journey.

Kenaz is like a torch that will lead you toward unlocking your creativity and self-knowledge. The light from this rune allows you to focus on your personal work. It encourages you to become your own individual to stand out from the rest of the crowd.

The light of Kenaz can cause you to experience a sort of awakening within yourself, thus resulting in personal growth. This rune will help you know how to create something from nature or inspired by it.

For instance, you can carve this symbol into the trunk of a tree. It will force the tree to grow into the shape of the rune caster's liking. It can also provide you with a stronger wood for whatever use you plan for it.

If you are an artist, you can apply this rune to all your creations. For instance, if you are a painter, preparing a base coat with the rune Kenaz painted into it will help guide your brush strokes. That way, they will follow what it is you intend to convey in your painting.

If you are cooking, stirring the pot in the Kenaz shape can help you think of that one unusual ingredient that will give your dish the perfect taste. Creating amulets inscribed with Kenaz will also help attract external forces to increase your strength, power, and creativity to higher levels. You can also use this rune whenever you want to improve your insight, letting you come up with brilliant ideas for your creations.

Gebo

Sound: "g"

Meaning: The rune Gebo symbolizes the gift of the process of giving to others. It represents the relationship between the giver and the receiver.

Gebo is the rune of hospitality, giving, and, most especially, of sacrifice. Although Gebo is the symbol for a gift, it is not about the item itself. It is more on the meeting point between the person giving it and the one who will be receiving it. Gebo speaks to partnerships between individuals. It also talks about honor, commitment, and hospitality.

Gebo influences you to sacrifice for your fellow men whenever they need help. It helps you become more capable of following through on your promises. It prevents you from backing down from your words, regardless of whether it is to a friend or refers to a business transaction. But you can also use Gebo to make others sacrifice for your sake, but know that it will often backfire on you.

Aside from that, this rune can symbolize the force of the exchange of vows between two people, like in a marriage. The exchange of gifts between the wedded couple brings joy to both participants. This joy increases exponentially when the gifts have the Gebo inscription within them. This rune will increase the chances of a successful union filled with health and trust between the two.

Charms and runes inscribed with the rune Gebo effectively attract and encourage the propagation of harmony between people.

Wunjo

Sound: "v" or "w"

Meaning: The last rune of Freya's aett, Wunjo, symbolizes joy and bliss. It encourages happiness and contentment within people.

With that symbolism, not surprisingly, why Wunjo is also said to be the rune of harmony, joy, and holistic healing. Casting this rune indicates luck and success in your endeavors. It also represents personal happiness and having friendly relationships with others. If you are going through rough times in your life, casting this rune during your readings is a good sign that good things are bound to happen.

Because Wunjo is connected to happiness and bliss, it makes it a useful rune when used in items such as gift wrappers or the gifts themselves. You can also use it when cooking for yourself and others. Just stir the pot using the shape of the rune, and it will imbue your dish with its influence.

If you are to manage a group of people or your household's head, the rune Wunjo can help you with your task. This is evident by the number of organized groups, like sports teams, schools, and clubs that use the rune to decorate their door frames, wall décor, etc.

When dealing with a group of people with varying ideologies and beliefs, it will take a lot of work to keep them in harmony. Using the power of Wunjo will make this seemingly difficult task more bearable. Another famous use of this rune is as a decoration to hang over your front door frame. The symbol of Wunjo will help you attract happiness and success into your household.

Chapter 8: Heimdall's Aett

Heimdall is the watchman of the gods. His task includes guarding the entrance to Asgard, which is the rainbow bridge, Bifrost. Heimdall is an ever-watchful warrior, and even though he is the sole guardian of Asgard against invaders, he does not waver. As a matter of fact, he shows unending courage. He has keen ears and eyes, patiently waiting for the time when he can blow his horn and signal the start of Ragnarok, which is the end of the world.

The second aett in the Futhark is Heimdall's aett, and it deals with the concepts of conflict and making changes. The first rune of this set, Hagalaz, is associated with Heimdall.

Hagalaz

Sound: "h"

This is the first letter in Heimdall's aett. Aside from being the rune symbol for the said god, it is also that of hail or hailstones, which also means destruction. This rune represents how our need or want of something can put a restriction on us. It restricts our possibilities but also contains the power we need to break free from those restrictions.

Hagalaz is one of the few runes that are almost entirely about destruction. It is also the rune for hail because it brings forth severe damage and natural destruction. However, not all types of destruction are inherently evil or negative. Sometimes, you will need to take down the old and non-useful ones to make way for the new.

For instance, storms or blizzards must blow away the dead branches of a tree so new growth can appear in their place. In addition, the dead limbs and leaves will serve as fertilizers for the tree and the other plants surrounding it, so they will grow taller.

If you get the Hagalaz run from a reading, then that means you should let go of the things from your past that may be hindering you from progressing further. It is like excessive nostalgia, which prevents you from making changes to things you are used to, even if you will greatly benefit from its results. One great way to use this rune is to make it part of a ward against natural disasters or bad weather.

Naudhiz

Sound: "n"

Naudhiz is the rune for necessity. It could be material gifts or anything intangible. Some also call this the rune of urgency, denoting that change is necessary, and everyone will need it soon. This rune's key concept is that it is nearing the time when you have to balance things in your life. You have to cleanse yourself and harmonize with the universe once more.

Naudhiz is the representation of how people's own needs and wants to serve as limiting factors to their growth. However, they also serve as the power that the same people need to use to break free from their restraints. It is all about how you use it.

This rune signifies the need to cut out the things in your life that hold you back and keep you from growing as a person. When you get this rune during a reading, it is crucial to reach deep within and ask yourself about the specific things you think you have to let go of.

Naudhiz also means using your unbiased thinking when making huge decisions in life. It may require you to let go of your personal biases and look at the situation from a bird's eye view so you can make a good decision. It is the best rune to use when divining for the perfect mate or partner. Moreover, it is ideal for spiritual and physical transformation that will lead to the perfect balance.

Isa

Sound: "i," "ee"

As the rune of ice, Isa denotes the standstill that blinds or impedes people from moving forward. These are the psychological stumbling blocks that prevent you from thinking or acting. It is telling you to turn inwards and examine the meaning of yourself.

Another meaning you can derive from the Isa rune is conflict resolution, denoting the need for mending relationships and/or clearing misunderstandings to move forward in life. You can also interpret Isa as conservation and self-preservation. It states you should look inside yourself to discover what you are doing that could limit your growth. It is saying you should help yourself first before you can do so for others.

Because Isa denotes conservation, it is good to use this symbol on your canned food or any other stocks you stowed away for later. The rune will help impede their aging processes, thereby giving them a longer shelf life. You can also carve this rune on the doors of your cupboards to attract similar energy.

Jera

Sound: pronounced like the "y" in "year"

Jera refers to the rune of harvest. It is also the rune that denotes the cycle of life. The key concept includes abundance. Just like when the harvest season arrives, every household has an abundance of food.

Jera represents the passage of time. It is the symbol of the cycle of the seasons and how it repeats all the time without fail. With the completion of one cycle comes growth, the fruition of the plans you have set into motion, progress, and your growth as a person.

However, Jera also has some negative aspects. For instance, this means you should expect retribution for any bad deeds you have done in the past. The reason is that everything always comes back full circle. It also symbolizes the repetition of negative behavior you should eliminate as soon as you can.

If you get Jera in your reading, then note it also means you will be seeing the results of your earlier efforts. It may be telling you you will be getting that promotion you have been working hard toward or finally paying off your loans.

If you are using the rune, you can carve it on the fence posts of your garden. By doing that, you will be blessed by bountiful harvests and protect your plants from disease and drought.

Eihwaz

$\int$

Sound: "eo" "ae"

This rune symbolizes the yew tree. It is also called the rune of endurance. Just like the yew tree, you can expect it to be more enduring the longer it stands. It can affect matters that require the use of consistent strength.

You can read Eihwaz as a quality of peak endurance that will not waver even when facing adversity. You can also read it as dependability. It is like someone who will be ready to help you even at his own expense.

Eihwaz also indicates that you are enduring enough; you are viewing obstacles in your path as steppingstones to reach your goal. You know how to fail upward. You are also patient enough to know how important it is to wait for the right time to make your move. This means you do not make hasty judgments.

However, there is a negative side to using this rune – that is, you may face a lot of confusion. The reason is that you will not understand what you should do next. It could also mean dissatisfaction, which can prevent you from feeling happy with the results of your tasks.

Because Eihwaz is the rune of endurance, it is best to carve this symbol onto the handles of tools you plan to use for many years to come. You can also turn it into an accessory to wear during rune crafting. It can help ensure that the ones you make will pass the test of time.

Perthro

Sound: "p"

The rune, Perthro, symbolizes the Dice Cup. It represents a dice cup tipped on its side, spilling the dice contained within and releasing the luck (or lack thereof) contained within.

It is also called the rune of gambling and taking risks. It is also more commonly known as the rune of mystery. It basically encompasses everything that is unknown in man's realm and the excitement of taking the plunge into a new endeavor.

It is also the rune that represents many secrets. Perthro is symbolic of the uncertainties and mysteries in life. It also symbolizes a mortal man's free will and the restrictions that come with it.

This rune has negative effects, though. Among these negative effects are delusions of grandeur, failure of risks taken, and generally all powers beyond man's control. This rune can also lead to overindulgence in gambling and delusions of winning the next hand every time.

To use Perthro outside of divination, you can stitch it into the gambler's wallet or purse. You can also put it in your logo if you are starting a new business. You can take advantage of the influence of Perthro in anything that deals with taking risks or trying new things.

Algiz /Elhaz

Sound: "zz"

Also known as the rune of protection, Algiz represents the Elk. It has a three-pronged design, which symbolizes the antlers of the stag. This rune represents the sudden urge of wanting to protect oneself or others from danger. It also means warding off evil and misfortune.

It has great restraining power, high defense, and protection. If you come up with it during your casting session, then you might need protection soon. Maybe someone you know can benefit from your protection.

Another definition you can read from Algiz is communication coming from the spiritual realm. It is like someone close to you who has been gone for some time is trying to talk to you or send you a sign.

If you get a reversed reading of Algiz, then it is highly likely there is danger lurking in the dark, or a sinister force is driving you away from the protection you are seeking. It may also indicate that someone will be turning his back on anyone who needs help. It is unknown which side you will be on.

In the olden days, warriors would carve the rune Algiz onto their shields for protection. In these modern times, though, when using swords and shields are out of fashion, you can just get a tattoo of the rune on your shield arm. It is your non-dominant arm, and it will provide you with the same form of protection.

Sowulo/Sowilu

ᛋ

Sound: "s"

It is the last rune in Heimdall's aett, which represents the sun. Many practitioners also call this the rune of power. Unfortunately, it was also the source of the Nazi's infamous Swastika symbol. This rune's definition can be extended to include clarity of thought, power, masculinity, and victory.

If you are seeking the help of this rune, you are asking for the ability to see with utmost clarity. It would be like the sun shining its light into the darkness to expose all that was once hiding in the shadows. This rune can also offer you guidance whenever you are figuratively in the dark with no idea what action you need to take to move forward.

Other readings you can glean from the Sowulo rune are good health, optimism, and confidence, among many other positive things. Basically, if you can come up with this rune during your rune casting sessions, you can somehow expect good things to come.

However, when you come up with the reverse of Sowilu, you can expect negative things like sudden, unexpected changes that can alter all your carefully laid out plans. It may also put you at risk of experiencing false success, not reaching the goal you set out to reach or gaining bad counsel you will most likely follow, unfortunately.

Historically, the Sowulo rune would be inscribed on stones that glorify the fallen soldiers. You can also use it as a sign to glorify Thor. You can inscribe this rune onto an amulet whenever you need additional courage to face adversity.

Chapter 9: Tyr's Aett

The god, Tyr, represents protection and complete victory. He is also the symbol of cosmic justice and all the things that relate to the politics of rulership. This aett concerns itself with intellect, spiritual growth, and understanding without judgment.

If you get a majority of the runes belonging to Tyr's aett during a casting session, then it could indicate that you are too inactive in achieving your goals. It could be you are overthinking your moves, or you are not centered because you are still uncertain of what you want.

Tir/Teiwaz

Sound: "t"

The first rune in Tyr's aett is coincidentally named after the god itself or at least a version of his name. It represents victory and justice, just like the deity. It is also called the Creator's rune.

Just like Sowilo, casting Tir usually promises success in your endeavor, but it may require you to make a personal sacrifice. Whether you will make a sacrifice or not will be the catalyst for your success. This rune also works well when embroiled in sticky legal matters, but only if you are in the right.

Just like the beginning of Heimdall's aett, Tyr's aett begins with a loss. However, it is a sacrifice you will do voluntarily. Unlike the hail sent down by the gods, the loss you will experience at the beginning of the third aett is under your control. You can get through without the sacrifice indicated, but this will be difficult.

However, to gain the benefits from the succeeding runes, make that sacrifice. Just like when Tyr had to sacrifice one of his hands so Fenrir, the gigantic and powerful wolf that was said to bring forth Ragnarok, could be shackled.

When you get a reversed casting of Tir, the consequences include loss of self-confidence, becoming an untrustworthy person in the eyes of your peers, and cowardice. In other words, you become the type of person who is weak, not just physically but mentally, and emotionally.

As mentioned earlier, this rune may help you sway the judge's favor toward your side, so carve its symbol on a small piece of wood. It should be small enough to fit in your pocket. You should then bring it with you to the courthouse.

Berkano/Berhano

Sound: "b"

This rune represents the Birch Tree. It represents a new beginning, like a birch coming to life from a similar tree from a seed buried in the soil. Berkano represents fertility and of having a home in complete peace and harmony. If you are planning to have a new member of your family, you can strive to gain the blessing of this rune.

It is also the perfect rune when trying to deal with concealment and secrecy. If you have something private and you wish to keep it that way, you may find the power of Berkano useful. The reason is that it ensures that you or anyone else will be spreading your secret around for everyone to see.

The Berkano is primarily oriented towards the feminine. However, you will notice it looks like a pair of breasts. It is a nurturing rune as indicative of it being oriented towards femininity. You can expect healing in both the physical and spiritual manner.

When cast in the negative, Berkano can cause secrecy within all household members, immaturity, and lust instead of fertility. In the worst-case scenario, a reversed Berkano may also signify abandonment.

To use this rune, you can carve it into a bedpost of a couple trying to conceive. You will also find it useful when placed in barnyard stalls where livestock are expected to bear their young.

Ehwaz

Sound: "e" as it sounds in "every"

Ehwaz represents the twin gods, the Alcis. You can often picture it as two brothers on horseback and linked by a wooden beam. This beam symbolizes the strong partnership between the twin brothers. It means that one cannot move without the cooperation of the other.

The rune Ehwaz is the Norse symbol for the horse, which represents partnership. As such, it deals with anything that concerns partnerships, like marriage, relationships, and business relations. Appealing to this rune will strengthen the bonds between the partners.

Casting this rune also means a new journey. For instance, you may be due for a job change soon or discover that you will need to move to a new home because of a job transfer. Just like the rune Tir, Ehwaz signifies a new start, but it may involve giving up something in return.

Another meaning you can divine when you cast Ehwaz is following the natural flow of a task you have in hand. It means learning how to work well with others instead of constantly butting heads. It also indicates learning how to depend on others, making it possible for you to accomplish all your tasks.

This rune's reversal may denote a couple of negative things, like treachery and reckless haste in doing tasks, which often ends in disaster. It could also mean breaking up standing partnerships.

In neo-pagan unions, the couple would paint the rune Ehwaz on their hands as a symbol of their everlasting partnership. They also do so as proof of trust and loyalty toward each other. And you can carve this rune on a plaque and hang it above your headboard.

Mannaz

Sound: "m"

It is the rune that symbolizes humankind. It can either represent your race or just you, the individual. This rune is incredibly special. You can apply it to situations and purposes that serve a social nature. It also helps strengthen bonds between the members of a group and develop a rational mind to deal with squabbles.

Casting Mannaz means undergoing self-analysis and inward reflection. If you find yourself stuck on a task and cannot seem to figure out what you need to do to advance, you can cast it hoping to find the answers to your questions.

Mannaz may also indicate the need to work on your personal reputation and people skills. Casting Mannaz when you have trouble working with other people may represent your desire to improve yourself instead of trying to find fault in the other members of your group. On the other hand, it can also mean you and your team have a strong bond with each other, and there is nothing you can't do when you work together.

Now, when Mannaz is in the negative, it may mean there will be a small problem that gets blown way out of proportion, negatively affecting your partnership. There are also instances when it signifies that you are unwittingly sabotaging your relationship and that your bond is getting weaker by the day.

You will do well to inscribe this symbol on your dinner table as that is where you and your family usually discuss family matters. It will amplify the bond you and your family share, leading to productive discussions.

Laguz

Sound: "l"

This rune represents the element of water and its flowing nature. It symbolizes the sheer power of water as well as its ability to follow the path of least resistance when it is flowing. Laguz is also symbolic of human thought and how you need to use it for good.

When you get Laguz from your rune casting, one way to read it is a safe harbor or place that offers you sanctuary from all the negativity in the world. Alternatively, it may not even be a place. It may symbolize a supportive partner or harmonious relationship you can count on when troubled.

Drawing a Laguz also indicates you were right to follow your intuition regarding any of your tasks at hand. Just like the flow of water, you let your intuition guide you toward the right path. You did not need to overthink and come up with your own obstacles. Laguz means you should let your unconscious mind take over occasionally as it may come up with a better idea.

A Laguz positioned in reversal, on the other hand, may indicate that you are emotionally manipulated, either by someone else who is close to you or even yourself. It could happen when you come up with excuses not to do something that is supposed to benefit you in the long run.

Carving this rune into an amulet or anything similar can aid in the further advancement of your mental abilities. It means you can learn even more. Another benefit of having a Laguz effect is that it can further enhance your intuition, making you much better at making decisions.

Inguz/Ing

Sound: "ng" as in the word "long"

Inguz is the Rune of Sexuality, which means it has power over physical attraction toward others, and ultimately, sex. This rune affects sex, but Inguz is only mostly concerned with the act in terms of reproduction and fertility.

Casting Inguz also means having the ability to spread your energy as far as you want to. It makes it possible for you to influence more people or provide more individuals with protection. However, to use the power of Inguz properly, it is important to build up your energy over time. Once you reach a certain level, you release it all at once.

During a reading, getting Inguz may also indicate the need to use more of your common-sense during decision-making if you tend to follow suit with what everyone else around you is doing without considering what could happen to you. Seeing this rune can help you figure out if you have to step back and use your common sense to realize that you are on the wrong path.

There is nothing much to worry about if you get a reversed Inguz rune during your casting, as it usually deals with minor inconveniences such as lust and immaturity. However, it may also signify decreased libido or infertility.

You can use Inguz in many ways aside from rune casting. For instance, you can carve the symbol on a piece of wood that is small enough to keep in your pocket. It will increase your chances of attracting a mate. You can also carve this rune on your bedpost to improve your sex life.

Dagaz

Sound: "d"

Dagaz, also known as the Rune of Transformation, represents a huge transformation, which might be of the spiritual, mental, or social type. Also called the Rune of Daybreak, it signifies the change between night and day, which is vast, to say the least. If you are seeking guidance when you need to make an important decision, Dagaz is one of the runes that can help.

Casting Dagaz also denotes the need to reconsider your current circumstance and whether you need to make a drastic change. It means you are questioning whether your decision is correct or not.

Another meaning you can get from Dagaz during a casting session is stability between opposing forces, such as light and darkness. You are getting hints on whether you need to certainly adjust to attain balance in your life.

The good thing about this rune is that it rarely has reverse effects. However, if the Dagaz rune gets surrounded by opposing, reversed runes, it could mean you have to look forward. You may also have to stop dwelling on the past too much.

Because Dagaz is the Rune of Transformation, it would work well when inscribed on the doors of a school or any other learning institution. Better yet, you should be able to find it in rehabilitation centers because those who are checked-in want to transform into much better versions of themselves.

Othala/Othila

Sound: "o" like in "old"

Othala is the Rune of Loyalty, which represents fealty to one's family, clan, tribe, country, or even cause/belief. Like Fehu, Othala is symbolic of wealth. However, unlike Fehu, Othala's wealth is intangible. This wealth is family, culture, heritage, and friendships. Othala represents a kind of enclosure and a way of maintaining the status quo.

Getting this rune during a reading usually connotes issues regarding your ancestry birthright. For instance, there may be something big going on in your hometown you would do well to at least inquire about.

This rune may also signify something related to your immediate family. For instance, a sibling of yours may want to reconnect after many years of not speaking. Another meaning might be that you will be called upon by your country or culture to lend your skills, like enlisting in the military. You may also work toward protecting your heritage soon.

Now, the most obvious negative effect of this rune is developing racism, bigotry, and general xenophobia. One unfortunate instance of the use of this rune was during World War II when Othala was engraved in the knives issued to the Hitler Youth members. Should you want to use this rune to gain its energy, you have to do so aided by something connected to family matters, like a family crest.

Memorizing the Futhark Runes

Now that you have learned about the three Aettir and the runes within them, you may be somewhat overwhelmed at how unfamiliar they are to you. It is understandable since you are essentially trying to learn a new alphabet.

However, there are mnemonic devices you can use to make it easier to implant the Futhark runes into your memory. One of the best and easiest ways to do so is to associate the symbol with their basic meanings.

First, let's tackle the first eight runes of Freya's Aett.

- **Fehu** - This rune means cattle, which connotes movable wealth. It has two lines jutting out from a vertical line, pretty much like the horns of a cow. Also, this rune looks like the letter "F," which it represents.

- **Uruz** - This means auroch, an extinct wild ox used to live in parts of Europe. Uruz represents primal power, and it looks like an upside-down "U." It is roughly the same as the profile of a bison or any other large land mammal.

- **Thurisaz** - This means thorn or thurs (giant), and it represents danger. It does look like a thorn. Imagine a stem with a single thorn jutting out the side. It also represents the "th" sound.

- **Ansuz** - This means as (a god), specifically Odin. It also represents Odin's domain, which is communication. This rune kind of looks like the letter "A." To remember it with ease, just associate it with the word answer. Coincidentally, Ansuz also represents the letter "A."

- **Raido** - This is the rune associated with travel. It may mean to ride a vehicle to get to your destination. Moreover, it looks like the letter "R," which it also represents.

- **Kenaz** - This rune means torch, which is a symbol of illumination and knowledge. Imagine a beam of light coming from a flashlight, starting from a small point and then radiating outward. This rune also looks like the letter "C," and it represents the sound of "c" or "k."

- **Gebo** - This means gift and has connotations pertaining to relationships and hospitality. It looks like the letter "X" and similar to the ribbon on a present.

- **Wunjo** - This rune means joy, and it looks like a pennant flag, the kind you would wave when your favorite sports team is winning the game. Speaking of winning, it also starts with the letter "w," which this rune represents.

These are the first eight letters of the Futhark. To remember the order of the runes, recite, "the Futhark is a gift of joy." The first six spell out futhark, while gift and joy are the meanings of the last two (gebo and wunjo).

Now, let us move onto the runes in Heimdall's Aett.

- **Hagalaz** - This rune means hail or hailstones. It represents huge changes or crises, much like the destruction left behind by a huge hailstorm. It looks like and represents the letter "H," which is the first letter in hail.

- **Nauthiz** - This means need, and it looks like how a person would rub two sticks together if he needs fire. It represents the letter "N" and has negative connotations for being needy.

- **Isa** - This means ice, and it represents stasis wherein everything is still, just like everything around you when it is winter. It looks just like an icicle and represents the letter "I."

- **Jera** - This rune means year (the "J" is pronounced like "Y"), and it symbolizes a year's harvest, something that you need to work for. This rune resembles two cupped hands ready to receive their hard-earned reward. It represents the letters "J" and "Y."

- **Eihwaz** - This rune represents the yew tree. Often, it also signifies the Yggdrasil itself. It symbolizes the mysteries of life and death. You can imagine the shape of the rune-like a sparse tree with one branch and one root. It also represents the sound "ei" (pronounced "eye"), which you can easily link to Odin, the one-eyed, who hung from the branches of Yggdrasil for nine days.

- **Perthro** - This means dice cup and symbolizes gambling and divination - two of the things where you can use a dice cup for. It is shaped like a dice cup tipped over. The name of the rune contains the sound throw, which is what you do with dice.

- **Algiz** - This means elk and the rune. With its three prongs, it looks like the antlers of a deer. The shape indicates a trident, which you can use for defense and keep enemies at bay. Remember the last letter of this rune's name because it also symbolizes the letter "Z."

- **Sowilo** - This rune means sun, and it represents energy and victory. Sowilo sounds like solar. It also looks like the letter "S," which it represents.

We have come to the end of Heimdall's aett. To remember the sequence of the runes, you can use the sentences "Hail needs ice harvesters. I was destined to protect the sun."

The first sentence consists of the meanings and associations of the first four runes. In the second sentence, "I was" sounds like eihwaz, and the rest of the sentence corresponds to each respective runes' associations.

Let's conclude with Tyr's aett. Here they are:

- **Tir/Tiwaz** – This rune's name is one version of Tyr's name. It represents honor. It resembles an arrow pointing upward, specifically towards the sky, and Tyr is a sky god.

- **Berkano** – This means birch goddess, and it is a rune of blessings and fertility. It resembles the letter "B" and represents it, too. Blessing starts with the letter "B," and so does the word baby.

- **Ehwaz** – This rune means horse, and it does look like the side profile of a horse, one with a saddle in the middle. When turned on its side, it looks almost like the letter "E," which it represents.

- **Mannaz** – This means mankind, and it is the rune of social order and awareness. It also looks like two persons with their arms locked in unity. It also resembles the letter "M," which is one thing it represents.

- **Laguz** – This means water, and the rune looks like the sail of a ship. The name laguz sounds like the word lagoon, which is a body of water. It also looks like an upside-down letter "L," which it represents.

- **Ingwaz** – This represents the god Ing (Frey), and it means seed. This rune symbolizes fertility, agriculture, and growth. It looks like vines that intertwine with each other while growing. The name of the rune has the "ng" sound, which is what it symbolizes.

- **Dagaz** – This means day, and it essentially means awakening or awareness. It also appears like the emergency alarm speakers, the kind that wakes you up and makes you jump into action. It also looks like two "D's" standing back-to-back.

- **Othala** – This rune means home, belonging, or inheritance. It resembles the roof of a house. Since it starts with the letter "O," it also represents that letter.

Now that you have memorized the eight runes of Tyr's Aett, here is a mnemonic device you can use to remember their order: "Tyr blesses horses and men; sail-ing all day back home."

Chapter 10: Odin's Rune

Aside from the usual 24 runes that compose the Futhark runic alphabet, modern neo-pagans and heathenry practitioners have introduced an extra blank tile in their rune sets and gave it the name Wyrd, which means fate.

Total emptiness or infinite possibilities? Depending on how you look at it, there are many ways through which you can read Odin's rune. This rune was a later addition by modern neo-pagans to get some additional chance from the cosmos when casting runes. Users of this rune say that when Odin's rune appears in your cast, it means that the unknown is at work and it is there even if you cannot see it.

Even though many rune casters use Odin's rune these days, its actual meaning is still hotly debated. Some say it means endless possibilities, while others say it indicates emptiness. It is like the glass half-full or half-empty conundrum.

What Does the Blank Rune Mean?

Whenever you get a blank rune, take note it could signify that you ran into some complications with your casting. It may be a hint that your inquiry is not worded properly, or it may be that the answer you are seeking is impossible to grasp (or maybe deep inside, you already know the answer). Take it as a sign you need to meditate and wait for before giving your reading another shot.

The consensus about Odin's rune is there is none. If you ask ten people about it, you will also get ten answers. There is no one definition of the blank rune. Any potential user can use it on whatever day they want to.

In his book "A Handbook for the Use of an Ancient Oracle" (1983), Ralph Blum said that the appearance of the blank rune is an omen of death. However, that death might just be symbolic and not an actual passing of a person. It can also refer to a certain part of your life gone and replaced by another.

According to Lisa Peschel, author of "A Practical Guide to the Runes: Their Uses in Divination and Magick," whenever this rune appears, the only thing you can expect is that something unexpected will happen to you. This something can be positive or negative depending on whether you have been virtuous. It is also best to interpret its meaning by basing it on how it relates to its neighbors.

Kylie Holmes, the author of "Pagan Portals: Runes" (2013), said that casting the blank rune indicates there is progress in your spiritual development. This act also reminds you how large your knowledge is. It is bigger compared to how other people view it.

In over a millennium of its existence, there have been very few modifications to the runic alphabet. These variations are usually geographic, and the shapes of certain runes were the only notable changes. Their meanings remained the same. However, there has been a modern addition to the Elder and Younger Futhark runic alphabet, and it is the Wyrd rune.

There has been no solid evidence that the Wyrd (also called Odin's rune) existed before the resurgence of using runes, and its origins are muddy, to say the least, but even so, it is included in most rune sets these days.

What Makes the Wyrd Rune Different from the Rest?

The Wyrd rune is often just a blank tile in the set, but some say it looks like this:

This rune symbol represents all the rune shapes molded into one. According to old beliefs, it is possible to make this rune by yourself aided by clay or any similar material. Regardless of your chosen material, it would be necessary for you to get a tiny pinch of material from the other runes to produce a new and blank one. It is the blank rune that serves as the culmination of all other runes' powers.

The blank rune differs from the others in the sense it does not belong in the three Aettir of the Elder Futhark. It is only a modern addition that originated around 40 years ago in the 1980s when the New Age revolution was just taking over Western culture. However, even though it is a new addition to the runic alphabet, most modern rune casters still widely accept it.

The blank rune is also distinguishable from the rest of the runic alphabet because it is mainly a part of an ancient alphabet. This means that except for Wyrd, every rune represents a sound or combination of sounds. Some practitioners say that Wyrd represents silence, making it a unique concept since you can find no alphabet in the world with a symbol for silence.

Traditional beliefs also indicate that blank runes existed for the sole reason of having a replacement tile if a loss occurs or misplacement of another tile. Purists also believe that the blank rune does not fit into the runes' mathematical and mystical system. The reason is that you can't merely divide 25 tiles into four (four seasons in a year, four cardinal directions, and others).

The Wyrd rune does not have its own set of definitions. You can even view it as total emptiness or infinite possibilities. Some also view it as a sign of unseen forces moving in the background to affect your fate.

Why is it Called Odin's Rune?

Another name for the Wyrd rune is Odin's rune, as it has unfathomable and mysterious power and meaning. Odin is the All-Father, the ruler of all the gods of Asgard, and yet he did not stop his quest for more knowledge. You can associate the blank rune with Odin, not only because of his omnipotence but also due to his constant hunger for more knowledge.

When Odin appears before you during a reading, he is calling out to you to look deep within yourself to achieve a deeper, more profound understanding of yourself and your being. The blank rune represents the human's almost unlimited potential, and it will be up to the reader how to take this knowledge.

It is also one reason Odin's rune does not belong in the Aettir. Odin stands alone, separate from the other aesir. Bringing any further meaning to Odin's rune would be like trying to tie a string around all the Nine Worlds. It would be futile and impossible.

How Should You Read the Blank Rune?

Although not all rune casters believe that the blank rune should be included in any rune sets, there is nothing that prevents you from using it if you want to. If you want to use Odin's rune in your readings, here are a couple of suggestions on how you can read it.

The early Anglo-Saxons, and many of the other tribal races hailing from present Northern Europe, believed in the universal force called Orlog, which means both "doom" and "destiny." Orlog oversees the fates of all the nations and their citizens. One way to read the blank rune is to base it on the concept of Orlog. This means that your individual fate is bestowed upon you by the Norns if you pull this rune.

The blank rune might mean you have karmic debt, and the cosmos is collecting payment. Now, your karmic debt might not be due to your past personal actions but from your past life. This may seem like it is unfair that you are responsible for what you did in your past life, but then again, it will also be the case for your next life. With that in mind, drawing the blank rune may mean you need to do better in your present life.

Another possible definition of the blank rune may be that you have reached a certain point in your life where you have reached the point of no return. You are destined to a singular fate soon, and you do nothing to change it. Even though you still have free will, it will not matter whatever you do now. The results will still be the same.

Now, if you pull out the blank rune in response to a specific question, it means it is not the right time for your query. It is like a Magic 8-ball telling you you should try asking again later. The cosmic fates may still cook something up for that part of your fate, so it will not register in the runes just yet.

Another definition you can get from the blank rune is that you will be experiencing huge changes in your life. However, because of the ambiguous nature of the blank rune, you cannot be sure if the change will be positive or negative. It could be getting a huge promotion and raise at work or losing a family member. You need to be careful if you seem to get a huge change in your life.

Should You Use the Wyrd Rune?

It totally depends on you if you want to keep the blank rune in your rune set. Purists might scoff at you behind your back if you use this rune. Some may even find it blasphemous that you even think of using a rune that was not a part of the Elder Futhark. However, using the blank rune will provide you with one that represents nothingness and how it can affect your life.

Also, remember that not everyone is as accepting of the blank rune, especially the purists, who see it as a sacrilegious abomination. They view the blank rune as an unwelcome product of the New Age lightheadedness and the ravenous appetite for sacred symbols. For them, a rune is a symbol, not an absence of it. A symbol for the absence of a symbol is not a concept used by the Norse. It is an oxymoron, and it contradicts itself.

However, despite many people rejecting the concept of the blank rune, it will be going nowhere soon. It is an idea ingrained in neo-paganism for 40 years. Through all that time, it has been enduring continuous scrutiny and dismissals from the community. It has become such a fixture it compels rune makers who choose not to add it to their sets for sale to mention it on their labeling. It happened even though the original set of 24 runes did not have it, and it was only introduced in the 1980s.

The question remains, should you use the blank rune? The final answer will always depend on you. If you want your rune readings to be as close to the ancient traditional rune reading, then avoid using the blank tile. If you are open to possibilities and are like many of the New Age neo-pagans, then there is nothing wrong with using the blank rune in your set. You can try using it when doing readings on yourself to discover if it fits into your reading style.

Now that you know what it is, how it came to be, and how to use it, you can form your own opinion about it. Whether you use it or not, it will not change that it is already in the mainstream rune reading scene and may continue to do so for quite a long time.

Chapter 11: Reading the Runes

Rune layouts and spreads can help you make sense of what they are trying to tell you. While each rune already has its own inherent meanings, you will need to know when those interpretations will come into play in your life. Using layouts and spreads will provide you with a structure designed to promote ease in translating the message of the runes.

What is the difference between layouts and spreads? You can't really find that many! If you are familiar with using tarot cards, you will discover that rune layouts are like tarot card spreads. Several rune casters use tarot card spreads when doing readings. In this sense, you can use layout and spread interchangeably.

Choosing which layout or spread to use is not that difficult. If you have only a simple question, you can use the layouts that use the least number of runes. If you have a complicated problem you need counsel for, a rune layout that uses more runes is in order. The more complex the problem, the more elaborate the spread.

Rune Casting Layouts

Here are some of the most commonly used layouts for casting runes:

One Rune Layout

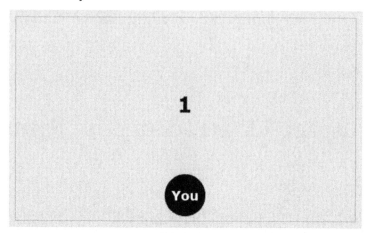

It is the most basic out of all the rune layouts as it only requires a single tile to read. You can either cast a handful of runes onto your rune cloth or pick the one that seems to call out to you. It is a great way to do a quick reading to help you with a sudden decision.

You do not even need to use a casting fabric nor remove your hand from your pocket. If you can read the rune by touch, you can get your answer in just a couple of seconds. It is possible to read this rune as your general feeling and attitude you feel toward the question. It also represents the outcome you will receive from the question.

Two Rune Layout

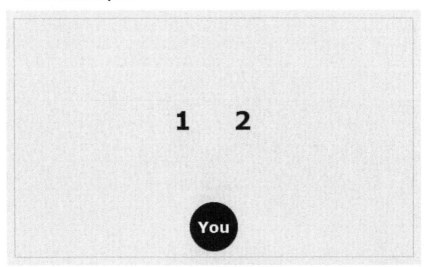

The ancient Germanic tribe believed that time has two aspects instead of three. For them, there are no past, present, and future. Instead, there is a "that which is" and a "that which is becoming."

The two-rune layout based itself on this two-fold concept. The first rune you pick out from your pouch will represent "that which is," while the second will symbolize "that which is becoming."

The first rune (that which is) includes the things that happened in the past and how it can affect the question asked. It will make you think back on your past actions. Did you really do something to warrant the cosmos to put you into the situation you are in?

The second rune (that which is becoming) encompasses the ways through which the events of the future, and the future, can affect the question asked of the runes. You might not be able to prevent any bad situations from happening. However, you can at least try to react differently to your reading.

Three Rune Layout (Past, Present, and Future)

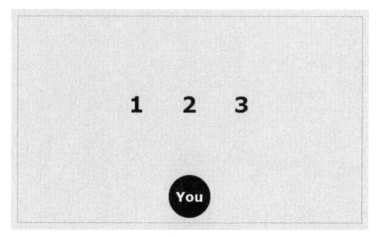

Not everyone agrees with the old Norse two-fold concept of time. You can use the three-rune layout to take advantage of the three-fold concept instead. The rune on the left, which is most likely the first one you cast, represents the past. But the middle is the present, while the one on the right is the future.

The past includes the events with a significant effect regarding the question. They are like the actions you did in the past that may be why you are in your situation.

The present refers to the things happening that affect your situation regarding the query. The future is just simply the outcome of the question you asked.

Unarguably, the three-rune spread did not exist during the ancient times when the Norse were still around. However, if this configuration speaks to you, no one can hold it against you if you want to use it.

Four Directions Layout

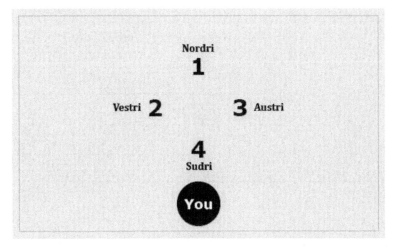

Because the runes came from Norse mythology, the four cardinal directions' names are named after the four dwarves that legends say are holding up the sky. It is made of the skull of the giant Ymir. The concept of this layout is simple. It is just a normal North, East, South, and West pattern with different meanings for each position, namely:

- **Nordri** - This represents the past, particularly influences that have effects on the past regarding your question.

- **Vestri** - This is the present, namely the things currently happening with an effect on the question that you asked.

- **Austri** - This represents the future and the possible obstacles you will encounter that might hinder the outcome of your tasks.

- **Sudri** - This is the total possible outcome of the reading.

There are things you need to know regarding this casting choice. First, it is like the three-rune layout because the past, present, and future are all involved. However, it is not the Austri rune that will predict the future for you. Sudri will take on the role played by the usual future position, instead.

Five-Rune Cross Layout

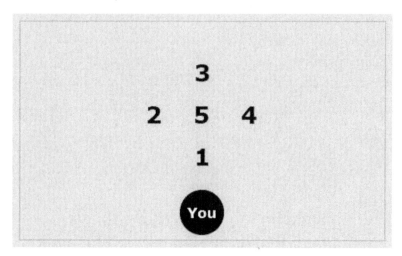

With this reading layout, you will be forming a cross shape with the five runes you have to cast on the cloth. The first will be at the bottom of the cross; the second will be at the left position, the third on top, and the last one will be at the center of the cross.

- 1 - It represents the general things that might be underlying in the question.

- 2 - These are the obstacles you will need to overcome to get your answer.

- 3 - It represents the beneficial processes you might experience.

- 4 - It represents the possible outcome/s.

- 5 - It will show the future influences that could affect the outcome.

Midgard Serpent Layout

This rune layout is based upon Jormugandr, the gigantic serpent known to encircle the world. Legends say that Jormugandr is so huge that he can wrap his body around the earth and bite his own tail.

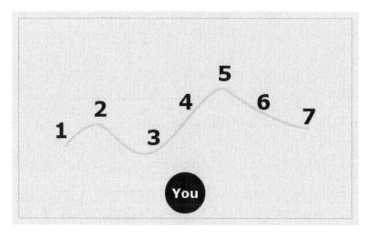

This is symbolic of how you need to be completely aware during the reading, or else the results of the layout might pass you by.

You will be setting up the seven-runes in a flowing pattern and imagine walking from the tail of the Midgard serpent up to its head. There will be a couple of uphill sections where you will be experiencing obstacles. However, note there will also be downhill sections where you can relax, making it possible for you to prepare yourself for the next uphill battle.

- 1 – It symbolizes your feelings in the past and their connection to the situation you are asking help for. Did you do something that resulted in your predicament?

- 2 – It represents the struggles that you have to go through because of your feelings from position 1. The hump represents the obstacles you overcame and that you need to know how you handled the past situation because it might come back to you in the present.

• 3 - This point represents your feelings about your situation. It is the rune nearest to your position because it roughly represents the present.

• 4 - It is the position where you start on your journey toward your desired outcome. The obstacles from the previous positions may come back to you. The hump at this position is also much steeper than the one at position 2, meaning the obstacles you need to face are more difficult than before. However, you now have the guidance from the past to help you.

• 5 - It is the peak of your journey where you can see your goal. This rune will show you your feelings and how they can control you when you think that your goal is within reach.

• 6 - It is the position that will remind you that there is still a bit more work to do before you reach your goal. You need to take heed of this rune the most. If it is telling you you need to put more effort, then do what it says. For instance, if you happen to cast a rune of power and control, you must be strong-willed and control your emotions until you reach your goals.

• 7 - It is the Midgard Serpent's head, and most of the time, it is the final goal. However, according to Norse mythology, Jormugandr could bite its own tail, so it is crucial to be mindful of what the runes are saying. Otherwise, you may find yourself back on the tail of the serpent.

Bifrost Layout

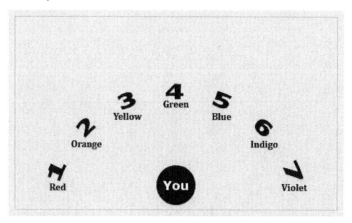

According to Norse legends, the Bifrost is the rainbow bridge that connects Midgard, the realm of humans, to Asgard, the realm of the gods. By using this layout, you will be getting a sense you are getting help and guidance from the gods themselves. You will be casting seven runes and place them in an arcing pattern, starting from the left to the right. At the start is the color red, and it will end with the color violet.

* **Red** - It encompasses your attitudes from the past that might have some effect on your inquiry.

* **Orange** - It represents the effects of the past that result from your past attitudes.

* **Yellow** - This rune represents your attitude at present with an effect on your question.

* **Green** - It represents the effects of your current attitude on the overall outcome.

* **Blue** - The rune represents what kind of attitude you need to have in the future.

* **Indigo** - It symbolizes the effects of the attitude in the future.

* **Violet** - It represents the overall outcome of your journey.

This layout might seem like a complicated one. However, if you examine it closely, it is still just a past, present, and future layout with a couple of exceptions.

Grid of Nine Layout

The Grid of Nine requires that you cast nine runes and lay them out in a grid, like the one below. Ensure that you follow the numbering shown, as it plays an important role in the reading effectiveness.

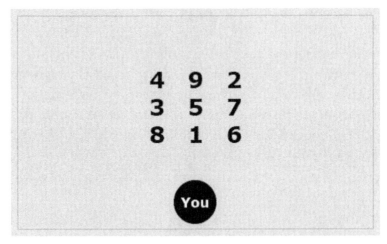

The special thing about this grid is that if you add the values of any row or column, even the diagonals, you will always end up with an answer of 15. To read this layout, begin with the lowest horizontal row first. This row represents the factors from the past that influenced the matter at hand.

- 8 – It refers to the hidden influences that happened.

- 1 – It encompasses the basic influences you experienced.

- 6 – It represents your current attitude towards the events from the past.

You should then follow it up by reading the middle row from left to right, including:

- 3 – These are the hidden influences that are acting at present.

- 5 - It will represent the current status quo.

- 7 - It refers to your attitude toward the things happening in the present.

Last, you have to read the top row as it represents the outcome of your inquiry. It consists of:

- 4 - This refers to the hidden influences, the obstacles that prevent the outcome from surfacing.

- 9 - It is the absolute best outcome of your question.

- 2 - It will show how you respond to the result.

Odin's Nine Layout

Odin, the All-Father, hung from the branches of Yggdrasil to gain the knowledge of the runes.

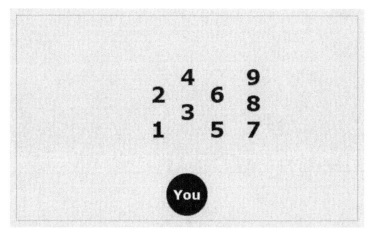

The first six runes represent Odin himself (1 and 2 are the legs, 4 is the head), and the last three are for Odin's spear. To read this layout, follow this:

The runes in the first column (1 and 2) represent the factors in the past that might have influenced your question.

- 1 - It symbolizes the hidden images that happened in the past.

- 2 - It is your attitude toward the past.

The column with the runes 3 and 4 represents the current affecting the outlet.

- 3 – It encompasses the hidden influences currently happening.

- 4 – It is the questioner's attitude regarding current events.

The column with the runes 5 and 6 will tell you about the answer to the question.

- 5 – This rune represents the hidden influences. It also symbolizes the causes of delay that may prevent the answer from manifesting.

- 6 – It is your response to the answer.

The last column (7, 8, and 9) represent the powers you either have or have to deal with. These figures represent the powers you have to take care of for the first, second, and third columns, respectively.

Celtic Cross Spread

Although this spread is usually used for tarot card reading, you can also use it for rune reading. You will need to cast ten runes from your pouch then lay them out in the same pattern as you would when reading tarot cards.

Before you cast, though, concentrate on the particular rune you would like help from. For instance, if you are trying to conceive, get a rune that represents fertility. Concentrate on getting it as you cast the ten tiles needed for this layout.

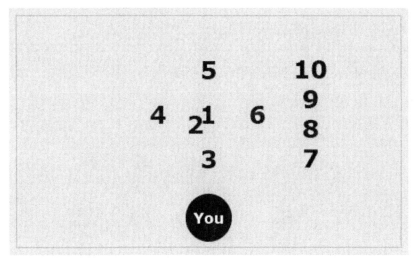

If possible, place rune number 2 over number 1. To gain understanding from this rune spread, here is how to read it:

- 1 – This represents the question at hand.

- 2 – It signifies the forces that might oppose your question.

- 3 – It covers the underlying influence that may affect the answer to your question.

- 4 – It shows the influences you are passing through or ending.

- 5 – It encompasses the influences that might become important in the long term.

- 6 – It represents the many influences you may come across soon.

- 7 – It refers to the fears and negative thoughts you may have.

- 8 – It points to the outside influences that can potentially influence the outcome.

- 9 – It refers to your beliefs and hopes.

- 10 – It will provide the best outcome for your inquiry.

This layout may seem a bit complicated, so to make it easier, imagine Odin standing in front of you with his spear held by his left hand.

Egil's Whalebone Layout

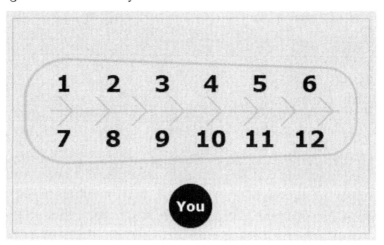

This rune layout took inspiration from the Icelandic saga "Egil's Saga," which is about a master poet, warrior, and runemaster, and his many accomplishments. There is a chapter in the saga wherein Egil cured Thorfinn's daughter Helga from an incurable disease. The reason Helga was sick in the first place included the wrong runes placed on her head. Egil removed the erring runes and replaced them with the new ones he carved into whalebone, instantly curing her.

For this layout, you will be doing something that differs somewhat from the other readings. Instead of each rune having a different meaning, you can group them by threes and read as if the group is speaking. It is basically a three-rune spread but doing them four times in one layout.

The four groups of runes derived their names from their purpose in the saga. Now, you do not have to read the entire saga before you can use this layout, but it can help. Knowing the story can help you remember what each group stands for.

Carver's Intentions (1, 2, and 3)

In the story, the rune carver had specific intentions for the runes. The first group acts just like that. You have a certain intention you want to consult the runes for. Before you cast the first three, think hard about what answers you want them to show you. Keep this intention in mind while picking out those that you intend to use. You need to keep this intention in mind while you are working towards the answer.

Helga's Results (4, 5, and 6)

Helga is Thorfinn's daughter, and she is the one harmed by the errant runes placed upon her forehead. For your purposes, this rune group will let you see the wrong results that could manifest if you have impure intentions or do not intend to put effort toward your goal.

Thorfinn's Concerns (7, 8, and 9)

Thorfinn is Helga's father, and in the saga, he worries about his daughter as she lays sick and dying on her bed. This group of runes is symbolic of the external concerns on your way to your goal. They can either be helpful or disruptive.

These outside influences can serve as support and help you on your way toward your intended goal. For instance, if your end intention is to become financially stable, these outside influences may come in the form of family and friends who help you when you are down in the dumps or help you find a more stable and higher-paying job.

The outside forces can also have a negative effect and may even hinder you from reaching your intended results. Using the example earlier of becoming financially stable, the outside forces may be your family or friends with ridiculous spending habits. They are influencing you to make irresponsible spending.

This group of runes will show you the things you need to keep an eye out for. Such could be helpful or destructive, and it will be up to you to discern which is which.

Egil's Results (10, 11, and 12)

Egil is the runemaster in the story. When he saw the runes, the state that Helga was in, and Thorfinn's concern for his daughter, he still made everything right again. Through his masterful skills of manipulating runes, he undid the previous rune maker's damage and made Helga healthy again.

This does not mean you need to recast your runes until you reach your desired outcome. This last set of three runes will only teach you how you can overcome the things you previously learned to achieve your goal. It also does not mean you can just disregard the previous three groups. It tells you how you can still reach your goal while remembering the possible difficulties that came from the first three groups. Think of the first three rune groups as a heads-up as to what you can expect on your journey so you can prepare yourself for the challenges.

The neat thing about rune layouts is that you have a choice whether to stick with the traditional ones (the one, two, three, or four rune layout) or make up your own. If you do the latter, make sure that it at least makes sense to you. The most important thing is that you use your insight to decipher what the runes are telling you based on the circumstances of the person asking the questions and the possible definitions, as stated by the runes themselves.

Chapter 12: The Poem of the Gods

Rune poems list down the letters of the runic alphabet and provide poem stanzas that explain each one's meanings. These poems were presumably made to be mnemonic devices designed to make memorizing them easily.

Three surviving ancient rune poems go back to the Middle Ages. The Icelandic and Norway rune poems were based on the Younger Futhark, while the Anglo-Saxon one is based on the Anglo-Saxon runes. Unfortunately, none using the Elder Futhark have ever been found yet.

Rune poems are more than just tools for memorizing the runes. You can also use them as chants to bolster the power inside each rune tile. It is also possible to use the poems to beckon and call upon the energies bound to each one, making your readings even more powerful than before.

Fehu

Wealth is won, and gold bestowed

But honor's due to all men owed

Gift the given and ware the lord

For thy name's worth noised abroad

In the older rune poems, one can see that money and its effect on relationships is vital. Money and wealth are important, but what you do with them is even more significant. Keeping money to yourself can lead to a reputation of being a miser. But grasping at what amount of money other people have will only lead to conflict.

Fehu is the rune of wealth, but it is also how you make and use it. It is about your community and how everyone shares whatever they can. It is about sharing your good fortune but also gracefully accepting help when you are in a bind.

Uruz

Wild ox-blood proud, sharp hornéd might

On moorland harsh midst sprite and wight

Unconquered will and fierce in form

Through summer's sun and winter's storm

Aurochs are wild oxen that once roamed the plains of Europe during the Middle Ages. It differs totally from the domesticated cattle mentioned in the previous rune Fehu.

In Runic terminology, Uruz symbolizes the unsurpassed will of explorers, the internal drive that allows you to set goals and achieve them. Without willpower, you become listless and insecure. It is the power you need to weather the storms that you are likely to encounter on your journey towards your goals.

In short, Uruz calls upon you to keep your focus and achieve the goals you set out for yourself. Also, it serves as a warning that there are multiple challenges on your path that will test your mettle.

Thurisaz

Thorn hedge bound the foe repelled

A giant's anger by Mjolnir felled

Thor protect us, fight for troth

In anger true as Odin's wrath

The thorn advises you to be cautious and aware of potential danger and challenges ahead. Unwittingly charge into thorns or grab a thorny vine, and you will pay for your lack of caution. If you fail to heed warnings, then you will pay for your actions.

You can also view thorns as protectors. For instance, keeping a hedge of blackthorn or hawthorn bushes will keep wild animals and certain human foes from invading your home.

Thurs, or giants, represent another kind of danger. These are often representative of the destructive and uncontrollable forces of nature. They can also be the forces within yourself that overwhelm you when you find yourself in a compromised position.

Ansuz

In mead divine and written word

In raven's call and whisper heard

Wisdom seek and wise-way act

In Mimir's well, see Odin's pact

Ansuz is the rune of wisdom. It is also the rune of listening to the voices that link you to the divine. Besides that, it represents being aware of the patterns of power and synchronicity around you. If you need increased wisdom or guidance or are just looking for the right words to say, invoke Ansuz.

Raido

By horse and wheel to travel far

Till journey's end a followed star

Harsh the road and sore the seat

Till journey's end and hearth-home meat

This rune represents traveling and the times when the journey comes with hard work, loneliness, and uncertainty of when it will end. Just like most journeys, they seem easy when planning for them. You will discover later that the road before you is full of obstacles and inevitable delays that will either make you want to turn back or power through them and grow.

Sometimes, the journey is about traveling and not the destination. The obstacles that block your way will also serve as challenges that will only make you stronger, but only if you do not give up.

Kenaz

Hearth and hallow, forging fire

Light the path and heart inspire

Torch of flame we hold on high

Guard the hall and burn the lie

Fire symbolizes dedication and transformation. It is also applying your truth, even if doing so comes at a personal cost. The same fire can also strengthen and empower you. It can provide focus and guidance. It is just like how a strong fire can temper and strengthen a sword.

Gebo

Lovers kiss and gift the hand

Lord's men shout and pledge to band

The gift is given back and thrice

In duty bound and honor's price

The gift-giver shows the receiver their appreciation. In return, the receiver is beholden to the giver, otherwise known as owing thanks. Gebo is the commitment between people. It is about trust, loyalty, and doing the right thing toward others. It is about putting your trust in other people and expecting them to do the same to you.

However, it does not mean that the receiver is technically the slave of the gift giver. There should be mutual respect coming from both sides. The receiver should give favor to the giver out of the goodness of his heart.

Wunjo

Harvest in and cattle fed

Table full and blessings said

Peace and joy in life be ours

With ease-full days and golden hours

This symbolizes the phrase, count your blessings. You need to focus on the good things you already have. They are gifts you need to enjoy wisely. Be thankful for the blessings you have and do not mind what you do not have.

Why would you fill your mind with negative thoughts when you can think of all the blessings you have received so far? You might even realize that you are at a better place in life than you first thought you were.

Hagalaz

Storm born hail as heaven's seed

Brings us pain and direst need

But ice corn melts in Solar's light

And waters crops in place of blight

Hagalaz can be read as a warning, but it can also serve as reassurance. Hailstorms do tend to be destructive, but thankfully, they are also quite short. And afterward, the hail will melt to water, which nourishes the earth. If some circumstances disrupt your plans, they often come with the seed for more benefits. More than anything, it is a lesson that will teach you to be more patient and accepting.

Nauthiz

This want constrains and binds the will

Yet drives us on to conquer still

Let need-fire burn when darkness falls

And summer seek when winter calls

Nauthiz symbolizes the fear of the unknown or what you would do if you found yourself where you feel trapped, and nothing seemed to go your way. This rune teaches courage in the face of adversity and creativity under pressure so you can keep searching for solutions rather than giving up.

Isa

Blue its beauty and smooth the way

But yet beware lest foot betray

As Niflheim's ice meets Muspel's fire

In Ginnungagap see Midgard spire

The rune Isa says go forward and take care but do not be full of fear. It also gives the promise there are good days still ahead. Winter may be cold and harsh, but it does not last forever, and it is not all gloom. If you take care and you know what you are doing, then the snow and ice hold a particular beauty.

It is like skating on a frozen lake. If you are careful and you take the necessary precautions, you will have a fantastic time. However, if you just jumped into the middle without taking care, you may just break through the ice and seriously hurt yourself.

Jera

Seasons turn, and sunsets follow

As seeds once sown are reaped the morrow

So harvest seek at summer's end

And till the soul for winter's mend

Jera is the rune of a certain kind of wisdom. It is the wisdom of growing old, letting go of some of your unattainable dreams, and embracing what will happen. Jera teaches people they should not fight their fate. What they should do, instead, is to go with the flow.

Jera teaches you not to fight against the current of life. It would be best for you just to relax and let yourself be carried by the flow. That way, you will reach your destination faster, and you will not be as spent as you would most likely become when you fight against the current.

Eihwaz

Yew bow drawn to guard the hearth

World tree spans a nine-fold path

From mystic tip where Eagle dwells

To Serpent roots, Yggdrasil's wells

Because yew trees have always been the tree of choice for graveyards and it is also poisonous, it has always been associated with death. However, that same poison is used by shamans to aid them whenever they want to travel to other worlds. It often leads them to answers they would not have access to otherwise.

It is not advisable for you to use poisonous yew to bring you closer to the gods as you may not be able to go back. Just invoke the Eihwaz and let it lead you towards enlightenment.

Perthro

From Urd's dark well is Orlog spun

Our past the path we have become

But life's womb still has choices yet

Until our doom and fate are set

Perthro is the mystery rune, meaning you cannot be entirely sure of what it represents. It is the rune of gambling, so the answer you will get will be uncertain. The cosmos have not decided on your fate, so you still have time to change it to however you want.

If you like to partake in some gambling (no judgment here, the ancient Norse like a bit of gambling as well), you can seek help from Perthro to guide your hand.

Algiz

Hands are lifted the Gods to praise

Blessings given to guide our ways

Protected be on ancient paths

Keep homelands whole, and safe our hearths

This is a rune that can help you when seeking divine intervention. However, you need to respect whatever hand is dealt to you and follow the path opened to you if you asked for it. You also need to invoke this rune if you wish protection upon yourself and upon your home and family.

Sowilo

Victorious shines the sky-shield wheel

By sailors watched to guide their keel

Shed healing rays and lift our souls

Give courage strong to win our goals

Sowilo, as a rune, is the one that challenges you, calling upon you to be courageous and as virtuous as you can be. Even though Sowilo is the rune of victory, you need to be actively participating in the battle if you wish to be part of the eventual victory. If you feel like nothing you are doing makes a difference in your life, implore the help of Sowilo to give you enlightenment and guidance on what you need to do.

Tir

A god's right hand for Fenrir's demand

Honour proved at the wolf's command

Tir defend us when all is lost

And teach us to give sacrificial cost

Tir is a constant reminder that even the gods will sometimes need to do the right thing to protect others, even if it meant that they need to sacrifice something in exchange. Tir is not just for justice for yourself. It also means you act just towards other people. It is doing the right thing even if you are not rewarded and even if it meant that you lose something.

Berkanaz

Birch mother goddess bringing hopes to birth

Show us our place and all nature's worth

Mystery enfolded and teacher of life

Keeper of doorways and Allfather's wife

Berkanaz is the rune of life cycles and the rune of the feminine and nurturing aspect. It will help show you your place in the natural order of things. Whenever you feel like you are lost and do not know where you belong, Berkanaz can help.

Ehwaz

Rider and ridden made one from the two

Both called together to work something new

Not earth bound but flying; spirit set free

So Odin rides Sleipnir along the world tree

The rider trusts his steed to carry him into danger and not buck him off its back, and the steed trusts its rider to protect it should the need arise. The rune Ehwaz is for close partnerships. It makes use of two energies combined to achieve something bigger than the sum of their parts. Ehwaz is about balance. It is about your skills and abilities taking precedence over your petty pride and selfishness.

Mannaz

To Ask and to Embla, to make humans whole

Ve, Vili, Odin, gifted blood, sense, and soul

Bound to the earth, yet filled with the other

We are joined in the life-boon, sister and brother

The rune Mannaz is about being human and how you use your gifts and honor them in everything you do. It also serves as a reminder that when you die, the gods can take your gifts away. It poses a challenge to the goals you set. Mannaz also calls upon you to become proud of your heritage as one being born of the gods.

Laguz

As leek grows from earth, bright green to behold

Wisdom and knowledge within will unfold

Water, the other world, spirit, and death

A doorway to pass through, beyond human breath

Laguz is the rune about water and anything connected to it. It could be a journey over a huge body of water, floods, and more. It is also about talking about your emotions, inner life, mind, and soul. It involves talking about your mental health.

Laguz also challenges you to contemplate death and the death of those around you, and not just the mortal body. Try to think about what happens to the soul when the mortal body perishes.

Ingwaz

Seed sown is rooted and nurtured for birth

New life beyond sight safe deep in the earth

Joy find in joining, sharing our pleasure

harvest and ploughing, each in true measure

The rune Ingwaz calls upon you to live your life as you wish and support others as they live theirs. This rune also celebrates the inherent potential in your life and everyone else's. You are your own person. You need not seek validation from others. You can live your life however you want to and treat others with the same respect you would expect from them.

Dagaz

To daylight from darkness, the circles return

Seeing the hidden, the wisdom we learn

Act now and surely, trusting thy heart

True flies the arrow, straight from the start

The symbol for Dagaz has two halves, which can possibly be interpreted as night and day. You can also call upon this rune if you need additional focus and the ability to concentrate totally and not get easily distracted by fear.

This poem speaks about the transition from night to day when the objects previously wrapped in shadows are becoming visible once more.

Othala

The greatest of treasures, more precious than gold

The gift to the young, passed from the old

As we tend to the roots, so the tree tip will flower

And sweet to the soul, the fruit of the bower

The rune Othala urges you never to forget your roots and where you came from. Also, you should never forget all the struggles you and your family had to go through so you could be in the position you are in right now. Othala challenges you to set aside your selfishness and always consider the greater community's needs before yours.

These poems are more than just simple mnemonic tools. All tell a story about the runes and their message. You will do well to memorize these verses and recite them whenever you are doing your readings. You will feel that you are closer to the divine. Besides that, your readings may even become more concise and accurate than they were before.

Conclusion

Now that you have reached the end of this book, you already know all the basic knowledge required to do your own rune readings. This knowledge should be enough for you to develop the ability to consult the runes yourself whenever you need some divine intervention or if you think you need advice on any aspect of your life.

Even though the ancient Norse is no longer with us in this world, their mystic arts are still present in these modern times. The art of rune reading is still alive and kicking today. Some might even say it is trendy. In fact, you will not find it hard to locate other like-minded people who share the same interest in runes as you do.

Part 2: Asatru

The Ultimate Guide to Norse Paganism,
Heathenry, and Asatru for Beginners

Introduction

Our beautiful universe is sacred and vastly diverse, and in this diversity it contains opportunities for limitless joy. Different tribes across the globe have their own belief systems and religions, which helped them make sense of their world. Further, the belief systems provide a moral and ethical framework for the followers to live a meaningful and fulfilling life in harmony with their community and nature.

Asatru is a religion involving the belief systems taken from old, pre-Christian Germanic traditions. Also referred to as "Odinism," it is believed to be the natural religion of the Indo-European (also called Germanic) people, before the advent of Christianity.

Asatru involves worshipping and paying tributes and offerings to the ancient Germanic gods, goddesses, deities, and other supernatural beings. A person who practices Asatru is called an Asatruar, and sometimes called a heathen too. Other names of Asatru are Germanic or Norse Paganism, Wodanism, etc.

Now, the above paragraph is only a tiny scratch on the vast and fascinating subject of Asatru. This religion and belief system goes far deeper and is believed to have its origins many thousands of years ago. While the subject is vast, the sources available on the subject can be mind-boggling. Various books speak in isolation about certain topics under Asatru, and many sources are comprehensive.

This book is written for someone who wants to get a better understanding of this marvelous subject—ranging from its origins right up to modern times. You will find everything you need to know about Asatru within the pages of this book. Nearly all your questions about Asatru will be answered here.

One of the best things about Asatru is that it is a great private religion. You can be an Astruar, and no one else needs to know about your beliefs but you. You are free to choose what attracts you to Asatru. And yet, numerous kindred groups all over the world offer you a sense of identity and connection with other practicing Asatruars. In the last chapter, you'll discover how to contact practitioners in your area and even learn how to start your own hearth.

This book contains that kind of information too, such as how to practice Asatru on your own, as well as how to find other practitioners and be part of a like-minded kindred group. The hands-on instructions on how to practice this belief system at home will give you sufficient material to start off immediately, even as you prepare yourself to become part of something larger.

So, read on and know that your fascination for Asatru is only going to deepen by the time you complete this book and understand its various chapters and elements described.

Chapter 1: What is Norse Paganism?

Norse Paganism is also referred to as Old Norse religion. It is the most common term used to refer to a branch of Germanic religion that grew and developed during the Proto-Norse period. Germanic religion or Germanic paganism is a collective term referring to the set of intricately connected religious traditions and cultures of the Germanic people from as far back as the Iron Age, right up to the spread of Christianity. Germanic paganism was an essential element of early German culture.

Understanding Norse Paganism, Its Roots, and Expansion

The Proto-Norse period, sometimes called the Viking Age, refers to around the first century B.C.E., when the Proto-Norse, an Indo-European dialect spoken in the areas in and around the Scandinavian regions, was believed to have evolved. During this period, the North Germanic culture formed as a distinct branch of Germanic culture. Christianity replaced the Old Norse religion between the 8th and the 12th centuries.

Old Norse religion is also referred to by other names, especially among researchers and academicians. These other names include pre-Christian Norse religion, Scandinavian Paganism, Nordic Paganism, Northern Paganism, North Germanic religion, etc. Written texts were non-existent or very rare.

Modern scholars have been able to reconstruct some aspects of Norse Paganism with the help of archaeology, historical linguistics, toponymy, and certain records left behind by the ancient North Germanic peoples like the runic inscriptions. Norse Paganism is classified as an ethnic religion and a "non-indoctrinated community-based belief system," considering that its customs, norms, and practices varied across time, societies, and geographies.

Followers of the Old Norse religion were polytheistic and worshipped and believed in a plethora of gods and goddesses who were divided into two primary groups, namely the Aesir, or "Æsir" in Old Norse, and the Vanir, both of which were equally powerful but were continuously engaged in battles and wars with each other.

The most famous deities of Norse Paganism were Odin and Thor. Other mythical creatures such as giants, land-spirits, and elves also inhabited the world of the gods, according to Norse Paganism. The central theme of Norse Paganism is Yggdrasil, or the world tree. In addition to Midgard—the home of mortals—there are multiple domains, including numerous afterlife realms, which populated the cosmology of Norse Paganism. Each of the realms has a controlling deity.

The tenets, principles, and codes of Norse Paganism were transmitted through oral culture and not in the form of codified or written texts. The Old Norse religion was rife with rituals, ceremonies, and rites. The priests and kings played an important role in performing public sacrificial ceremonies and rituals.

In ancient times, these rituals were performed outdoors in places such as lakes and groves. By the 3rd century C.E., buildings and houses were specifically constructed for these ceremonies. A form of sorcery called Seiðr, which is closely linked to Shamanism, was practiced in the Old Norse religion. The funeral ceremonies of Norse Paganism were quite elaborate. Both cremations and burials were used in the culture and invariably included numerous grave goods.

Right through Norse Paganism's history, vast amounts of trans-cultural diffusions took place, especially with the neighboring cultures. A couple of examples include the Finns, the ancient followers of Finnish Paganism, and Sami, an ancient polytheistic and animistic tradition that, according to anthropologists, is also closely related to Shamanism. The diffusion and variations are largely attributed to the lack of codified texts and dependence on oral transmission of belief systems.

During the Viking Age, the Norse followers from different regions and cultures were more or less a unified entity, thanks especially to the shared Germanic language called Proto-Norse or Old Norse. During this time, Norse Paganism shared ideas and concepts across other cultures, traditions, and languages, which were conditioned by similar ecological, geographical, and cultural factors.

Ethnocultural groups influenced Norse Paganism of the Viking Age through similar traditions, languages, and geographies like:

Balto-Finns – Inhabiting the Baltic Sea region in northern Europe, the Balto-Finns are also referred to as Baltic Sea Finns or Western Finnic peoples. They speak Finnic languages.

Sami – The Sami peoples inhabit the Sapmi region, which forms present-day Sweden, Norway, the Kola Peninsula, and Finland. The Sami people have been commonly referred to as Lapps or Laplanders, a term that is seen as offensive by some Sami people. Therefore, only Sami is used among modern-day scholars.

The ancestors of the Sami people were from the Volga region, Russia, and other Uralic geographies. The Sami people's language is collectively known as Sami languages, a branch of the Uralic language family.

Anglo-Saxons – The Anglo-Saxons lived in England right from the 5th century. This cultural group consisted of Germanic tribes who migrated from continental Europe to England. Their descendants, and other indigenous tribes of England, adopted and imbibed a lot of Anglo-Saxon culture and language. The Anglo-Saxons established the Kingdom of England and helped in growing and developing the English language, which owes a large percentage of words to the language of the Anglo-Saxons.

Greenlandic Inuit – The Greenlandic Inuits are the indigenous people belonging to Greenland and speak the Greenlandic languages, including Kalaallisut, Tunumiit Orassiat or East Greenlandic, and Inuktun or Polar Inuit.

Norse Paganism was completely routed out of existence by Christianity in the 12th century, but some elements were retained as part of the Nordic folklore. Before the advent of Christianity, the practitioners of Norse Paganism did not see the belief system they were following as a religion but more as a way of life, which was incorporated into their daily lives in the form of behavioral attitudes, actions, and rituals. Christianity's arrival generated a conscious need to distinguish the ancient Norse Paganism as a religion separate from Christianity.

Textual Sources for Norse Paganism

Considering Norse Paganism depended far more on oral transmission of its culture and traditions rather than codified texts, very few textual sources are available. Some runic inscriptions survived from Scandinavia. These inscriptions are clearly religious in nature as they contain prayers to Thor, one of the most important Norse gods, to protect objects such as memorial stones. Thor's hammer can also be seen carved in these inscriptions.

While runic inscriptions that have survived the vagaries of time are very few, a considerably large body of historical and religious sources is available. All these texts are Old Norse manuscripts but written in Latin, reflecting the fact that these were codified after Scandinavia was converted to Christianity.

For example, Hávamál is a collection of Old Norse poems transmitted orally right from the Viking Era. According to Norse Paganism, this work contains poems, morals, and ethics, including ritual obligations. Sagas are another form of Norse literature, which contain information about pagan practices and beliefs.

A classic example of a historical saga related to Norse Paganism is Snorri Sturluson's *Heimskringla* and the *Landnámabók,* both of which talk about the early history of Iceland. Snorri Sturluson was an Icelandic poet, politician, and historian of the 12th century who has authored many books and retellings of oral Norse mythology and pagan practices and beliefs. *The Sagas of Icelanders* are prose narratives that have information about Icelandic groups, tribes, and important individuals in Iceland's history. Skaldic poetry is another important literary source that gives us information about the Old Norse religion.

Christians recorded these works of Norse literature, and they were passed on orally until the 12th century, which is when doubt arose about whether they were still accurate representations of ancient Norse Paganism. Most of the Christian chroniclers are believed to have taken a hostile view of the Old Norse religion. Therefore, modern scholars regard these literary sources more as historical fiction rather than verifiable historical records.

Literary sources from regions other than Scandinavia also exist. For example, *Germania,* dating back to around 100 C.E., was written by one of the greatest Roman historians named Tacitus. This book describes the religious beliefs and practices of numerous Germanic tribes.

Toponymic and Archeological Evidence

Considering that most textual sources are seen as historical fiction, archeological and toponymic evidence play an important role in understanding Norse Paganism. Archeological excavations of cult sites and burials especially give us important information about Old Norse religion and culture before conversion to Christianity.

Toponymic evidence relates to place names. For example, names of places with -hof, -horgr, -ve, etc., are typically sites of religious activity. Magnus Olsen, a Norwegian professor of Norse philology at the University of Oslo and linguist of the 20th century, developed a typology of placenames in Norway. He used this system to discover pagan worship places in Norway that included fields, groves, and temple buildings.

Expansion of Norse Paganism

During the Viking Period, Norse people left Scandinavia and settled through northwestern Europe. In the 9th century, they colonized Iceland (a sparsely populated region) and spread their belief system. According to toponymic evidence, Thor was the most popular deity in Iceland, whereas Odin doesn't find a place of prominence. Saga sources suggest the Icelandic settlers worshipped Freyr too.

The Norse people brought their Old Norse religion to Britain around the end of the 9th century. Again, toponymic evidence comes into play here. For example, Roseberry Topping is a site in North Yorkshire. This place was called Othensberg (or Óðinsberg in Old Norse language), "Hill of Odin," in the 12th century. Other place names had references to Norse mythological elements such as alfr, skratii, and troll.

Around the 19th century, there was a revival of interest in Norse Paganism when its various elements, characteristic features, and more, inspired artworks in the Romanticism movement. Around the same time, a lot of academic research work began on the topic, too, thanks to the interest from the art world.

Beliefs of Norse Paganism

Norse mythology consists of stories about Norse gods, goddesses, and deities, which are presented in Eddic poetry. Norse Paganism was a polytheistic culture, and believers prayed to various deities who lived lives similar to human beings, including expressing emotions, marrying, having children, and even dying. For example, Baldr, one of the Norse gods and a son of Odin, dies too.

Not all Norse deities were worshipped. For instance, Loki was an important god in Norse mythology, but there is no evidence of people worshipping him. Though, with new archeological discoveries, new knowledge may come to the fore. It is most likely that the community and the region where people lived directly affected how the different gods and deities were worshipped. Also, each individual treated the gods and goddesses differently. For example, in one skaldic poem of the 10th century, Egill Skallagrimsson describes Odin as a vinr or fulltrui (friend or confidant).

Mythological sources describe two types of deities, namely the Aesir or Æsir, and the Vanir. These two classes of deities fought a bitter war with each other, which ended through a truce and the freeing one another's hostages. The important Æsir deities are Thor, Tyr, and Odin. Some Vanir deities of importance are Njǫrðr, his daughter Freyja, and his son Freyr. Loki's status among this pantheon of gods is not very clear, although Snorri explains that he is buried under the Earth until Ragnarok, a calamitous world event where great wars will be fought, natural disasters will take place, and the world will be submerged in water.

Norse mythology describes deities who originated from giants. Some of these deities are Skaði, Rindr, and Gerðr. Interestingly, the word for goddesses in the Old Norse language is Ásynjur, which is just the feminine version of the word, Æsir. This interpretation could be the reason behind the myth, even though the two classes of deities were equally powerful. Some scholars believe that another Old Norse word for goddess could be dis. This word is used to refer to a collection of female supernatural beings.

Other beings described in Norse mythology include:

- The Norns – female deities who decided people's fates.
- The vættir – land spirits who occupy trees, mountains, waterfalls, rocks, rivers, etc.

Also, there are mentions of levels, dwarfs, guardian spirits, and other deities, many of whom have uncertain stature in the hierarchy. In addition to the above deities, Norse Pagan followers also worshiped local and ancestral spirits and deities. The Finns and Sami people venerate their ancestors through ancestral spirit worship. In some Norwegian tribes, every family had a dedicated family deity.

Cosmology in Norse Paganism

Cosmogonies or creation myths abound in the surviving texts of the mythologies of Norse Paganism. These stories are rife with Nordic gods, goddesses, and other elements.

According to Nordic mythology, before the creation of the universe, there was only a void called Ginnungagap. A giant named Ymir appeared first, after which multiple gods emerged from the void. These gods lifted the earth from out of the sea. Another version of the Nordic creation story talks about the world being created from Ymir's body. His flesh became the earth, his bones became the mountains, his skull was made into the sky, and his blood became the sea.

According to Snorri Sturluson's *Gylfaginning,* the void Ginnungagap existed. Two realms emerged from this void, including the fiery Muspell and the icy Niflheim. Surtr, the fire giant, controlled Muspell. These realms produced a river that coagulated to form Ymir's body. A cow named Audumbla provided Ymir with milk. The cow also licked a big block of ice to free Buri. Buri's son Bor married Bestla, a giantess.

The Yggdrasil, or the cosmic tree, is described as a giant ash tree with three roots, which are home to the goddess Hel, frost-giants, and human beings. Yggdrasil translates to "Odin's Steed." The story of Ragnarok reflects the idea of an inescapable destiny that Nordic people believe in.

Afterlife in Norse Paganism

The Old Norse religion has fully developed concepts of the afterlife. According to Sturluson, there are four realms that the dead people are welcomed into. Interestingly, Norse Paganism did not believe that the morals followed in human life would impact the individual's destination to his or her afterlife.

Warriors who died in battle were taken to Valhalla, Odin's hall, where they waited until Ragnarok when they would battle with the Æsir. Those who died from old age or disease would go to Hel. The other two afterlife realms mentioned by Sturluson were the hall of Brimir and the hall of Sindri. Some Eddic poems talk of the dead living in their graves, remaining conscious there.

The Norse god Odin is most closely associated with death, especially death by hanging. There is a reference to Odin in *The Poetic Edda* to this effect. Odin hanged himself on Yggdrasil for nine nights to gain magical power and wisdom.

The Decline of Norse Paganism

The Nordic people learned about Christianity when they settled in various parts of Europe, including the British Isles, Byzantium (present-day Constantinople), and Novgorod (one of the oldest historic cities in Russia). Therefore, when Christianity came to Scandinavia, it was already an accepted religion. Thus, both Scandinavian migrants and those who remained at home were converted to Christianity very early on, often encouraged by the ruling kings who embraced, patronized, and allowed preachers to convert and spread the new religion.

By the 12th century, Norse Paganism was almost entirely forgotten by the Norse people, although mythological stories survived through oral transmission until the 13th century when they were recorded in written form. Although it is not clear how these old belief systems were passed down orally, scholars believe that there was the possibility of little pockets of pagan believers that retained their belief systems right through the 11th and 12th centuries.

Although the Norse people converted to Christianity, most of them continued to use their mythological motifs and elements in many social and cultural contexts, which ensured that Norse Paganism remained a part of the regional culture and traditions. Norse gods continued to make their presence felt in Swedish folklore as well.

Snorri Sturluson was an important contributor to this revival movement in the 12th century through his skaldic poetry guide called *Prose Edda*. Visual records of Norse mythology are found in picture stones in Gotland. Many visual records include Norse elements as well as Christian elements such as crosses, reflecting an era of the synchronization of Norse Paganism and Christianity.

The Concept of Paganism

It makes sense to understand how the term "paganism" originated and how its meaning has changed over time, considering that we are talking about Norse Paganism. The word "paganism" comes from the Latin root word "paganus," which means civilian, rustic or rural. It was first used in the 4th century C.E. to denote people who followed polytheism. The word was also used for those people whose cultural beliefs included ritual sacrifice.

Paganism in the modern world incorporates practices and beliefs inspired by the ancient world, especially nature worship and animism, and yet it is different from the world's various religions. In the book *A History of Pagan Europe* by Prudence Jones and Nigel Pennick, pagan religions have the following characteristics:

- ***Polytheism*** – Paganism recognizes multiple gods, goddesses, and divine beings.

- ***Nature-Worship*** – Most pagan religions believe in the divinity of nature and worship elements of nature.

- ***Sacred Feminine*** – Another common trait of paganism is the recognition of the female divinity, often referred to as "goddess."

Initially, paganism was used in a derogatory way and implied a sense of inferiority. It was considered to be any religion or belief system followed by rustics and peasants. Slowly, the term began to mean any unfamiliar religion, but in the modern age, the term paganism has changed and has evolved to include new terms as well, such as Polytheistic reconstruction, Neopagan movements, and Modern Paganism.

Chapter 2: The Old Ways – The Vikings and the Anglo-Saxons

Norse Paganism, Vikings, and Anglo-Saxons are closely interconnected. This chapter is focused on the Vikings and the Anglo-Saxons.

Viking Paganism

Vikings are usually seen as barbarians, raiders, and heathens, a perception created by the religious writers of the Medieval Period. But these ideas are slowly changing today, thanks to new archeological discoveries being made. This group of Nordic people had much more to them than this simplistic depiction. The Vikings lived a life of sophistication and had their own set of traditional practices and belief systems. They were excellent warriors too.

Originating from present-day Sweden, Norway, and Denmark, Vikings started migrating toward coastal Europe around the end of the 8th century. They began as small bands of raiders conducting raids on little villages and slowly expanded into large armies consisting of thousands of soldiers, warriors, and fighters. Here are some interesting Viking facts, belief systems they followed, and a few debunked myths too.

Vikings Were Not Unclean Savages – Vikings are often depicted as unclean and barbarous savages. In truth, they were cleaner than most of the other European tribes they conquered. The Vikings loved to take showers, and this fact is interesting considering that at that time, many tribes were disdainful about regular bathing for the sake of cleanliness. Vikings had a special day referred to as "laurdag" where the Viking people took long, elaborate showers and used accessories such as combs for cleaning.

The Vikings Were Excellent Boat Makers and Sailors – The Vikings were highly successful in conquering many regions along the European coast, which reflected their excellent ability to make boats and sail. In all the Viking raids, they used speedy longboats, empowering them to travel at great speeds.

Also, these longboats allowed the Viking conquerors to enter shallow waters and get close to the land, giving them the advantage of swiftly conducted raids similar to hit-and-runs. The Vikings excelled at making these fast longboats that served their purpose well.

Viking Warriors Killed in Battle Went to Valhalla – According to the Vikings, warriors who were killed in battle were not sent to the regular afterlife. They were sent—actually carried by mythical female beings or valkyries—to a special place called Valhalla, in Asgard. Odin looked after these slain warriors, giving them a life of luxury, and prepared them for Ragnarok, the Viking concept of the end of the world.

Vikings Were Family and Community-Oriented – Vikings are shown as being a savage tribe with no family, community, or social laws. This myth has also been busted, since it is now known that the Vikings had an event called the "Thing" (as translated from the Old Norse language). This special event was conducted to keep law and order and settle legal disputes.

Crimes such as theft were settled, and sentences passed on to the parties found guilty, much like the current legal system. The decisions reached in the special event were considered ultimate with no further appeal, and everyone in the tribe, including the powerful people, had to abide by them. Occasionally, women were allowed to attend this event to express their opinions.

The fact that the Vikings played ice sports also speaks to their community-based living. Vikings turned their ice-cold and snowy regions to their advantage by playing multiple snow-based games and sports. Some scholars believe that the Vikings may have been the first to ski and skate on ice. They also played a sport called knattleikr, resembling modern-day ice hockey.

The Concept of Divorce Existed in Viking Society – Women were allowed to participate and express their views during the "Thing" and had multiple privileges and rights, most of which were not part of contemporary European tribes the Vikings conquered. For example, Viking women had property and divorce rights.

If the man didn't run his household and/or farm well and could not provide for his family, the wife could approach the concerned people in power for a divorce. Other reasons for divorce included physical and mental abuse. In fact, divorce was an easy process to follow, as well. The concerned party just needed two witnesses and to state that she was divorcing her spouse. This procedure had to be repeated in two places, one was a public place outside the family home, and the second was within the home near the nuptial bed.

Some of Our Weekdays Are Named after Viking Gods – Many scholars believe that a number of our weekdays are named in honor of Viking gods. For example, Thursday is believed to be an Anglican form of "Thor's Day," the Norse god of thunder and lightning. Scholars also believe that Wednesday is named after Wooden, which is another name for Odin. Tyr inspires Tuesday, and Friday is named after Frigg.

Belief Systems of the Vikings

The Vikings believed in numerous gods and goddesses who were elaborately described in Norse mythology. Vikings were followers of Norse Paganism. There were little, or no written sources or codified texts representing the Old Norse religion during the Viking Age. Along with the belief in a number of gods, goddesses, and divine beings, the Vikings also practiced multiple traditional rituals and rites, especially during special occasions and events to commemorate them.

The most important deities of Norse Mythology included Thor, Odin, Heimdall, Loki, Balder, Tyr, and Frigg. Each of these divine beings was associated with certain elements or things, and each of them had unique functions and powers too. For example, Thor was the god of thunder and lightning.

Vikings believed in two tribes of gods, namely Aesir and Vanir. Odin, Thor, Frigg, Balder, Loki, and others belonged to the Aesir tribe. Odin was the chief god as well as the god of wisdom, death, war, and property. His wife was Frigg, and she was the goddess of marriage and motherhood. Thor, the most powerful among the pantheon of Viking gods, was Odin's son and the god of thunder, lightning, and storms. Loki was considered to be a powerful but unpredictable god who gave birth to many evil beings and creatures.

All the gods and goddesses played important parts and roles in Norse mythology. The various details and stories of the pantheon of gods and goddesses of Norse Paganism are contained in Norse mythology, along with creation myths and conflicts between gods and humans, gods and heroes, and many other tales. According to Norse mythology, our cosmology, consisting of many worlds and realms, is centered on Yggdrasil's cosmic tree.

Rites and Rituals – Vikings believed in and commonly practiced sacrificial rites and rituals. They sacrificed different animals like cows, roosters, hens, and dogs. Even human sacrifice, especially the slaves of Vikings, was a common occurrence in the Viking Age. Human sacrifices took place at specific religious locations and/or temples.

So why and when were sacrifices performed by the Vikings? Sacrificial rituals were performed in honor of various gods and goddesses and on special occasions. For example, sacrifices were conducted before the Viking warriors set out for battle or set out on a journey, especially sea voyages, and even after completing a deal. Also, sacrifices were typical rituals during certain ceremonies such as marriages and funerals.

Marriage Ceremonies Among the Vikings – Marriages were an important aspect of Viking culture and tradition. Often, preparations for marriages would take up to three years because the concerned families needed to settle dowries, property transfers, and inheritances through the marriage. Marriages were grandly celebrated, and festivities could go on from three to seven days.

Friday was considered an auspicious day for marriages because it honored the goddess of marriage. An important event during the marriage was the handing over of the family's sword (usually passed on for generations) by the groom to his bride. She would hold it safely until she could pass it on to their son. In return, the bride passed her father's sword to the groom as a symbol of transferring her guardianship from her father to her husband.

Role of Magic in Norse Mythology and the Viking Culture – Magic was a potent element of the Vikings' belief system. They were predisposed to different forms of superstition. The Vikings believed that Odin discovered the power and wisdom of magic. He is believed to have invoked a volva (a class of powerful Norse witches) to get some questions answered. Interestingly, Norse mythology depicts mostly feminine figures practicing magic, driving the idea that magic was a feminine prerogative.

Temples of the Vikings – Vikings constructed temples for their gods, goddesses, and deities, including Odin and Thor. Often, temples were used for rituals and sacrifices. Numerous large mounds found all over Scandinavia are believed to be sites of Old Norse temples. Also, scholars believe many of the temples were demolished and replaced by churches later. As of today, no Viking temples survive.

Viking Burials – Multiple archeological evidence points to the fact that the Vikings believed in the concept of an afterlife and equipped the dead accordingly. Dead bodies were buried along with many items, including jewelry. Burials were elaborate ceremonies that often included sacrifices as well. Human sacrifices of slaves were often performed because the Vikings believed the slaves would accompany the dead person in the afterlife.

The Decline of Norse Paganism Among the Vikings – When the Vikings started attacking and conquering the European coasts at the end of the 8th century, they were exposed to Christianity. Most of the Vikings that set out to conquer these regions settled in these parts of Europe, including Normandy, Ireland, and Britain. The settlers slowly started accepting and adopting the tenets of the new religion until, eventually, most of them converted to Christianity.

Soon, Christianity spread to Scandinavia too, and by the end of the 12th century, it was firmly established in the Viking strongholds of Sweden, Denmark, and Norway. With the acceptance and increasing popularity of Christianity, Norse Paganism began to decline. Some of the ideas were lost, while others were merged into the new religion.

Anglo-Saxon Paganism

Anglo-Saxon paganism refers to the old belief systems and practices followed by the Anglo-Saxons between the 5th and 8th centuries. Anglo-Saxon paganism, also referred to as Anglo-Saxon traditional religion and Anglo-Saxon pre-Christian religion, consisted of a variety of cultic beliefs and practices from different geographical regions.

Believed to be an Iron Age religion, it was introduced to Britain by the migrating Anglo-Saxons (distinct from Roman-British peoples) from Germanic regions in the mid-5th century. They brought their culture and belief systems to Britain, which remained dominant until Christianity's consolidation around the 8th century.

Our knowledge about the pre-Christian Anglo-Saxon paganism comes to us from textual sources, especially those written by Christian Anglo-Saxons like Aldhelm and Bede. Other sources that build our knowledge of these times are archeological evidence and toponym or place-names. This polytheistic belief system had a central theme of deities referred to as ése (singular ós), which was a word for God in Old English.

Place names such as Easole, which translates to God's Ridge (in Kent), and Eisey, which translates to God's Island (in Wiltshire), gives us toponymic evidence of old Anglo-Saxon religion. Woden, or Odin, gets the maximum exposure in this belief system. Examples of Anglo-Saxon paganism through place names include Woodnesborough, which means Woden's Barrow in Kent, Wansdyke or Woden's Dyke in Wiltshire, and Wensley or Woden's Wood in Derbyshire.

Interestingly, Woden comes as an ancestor of Wessex, Kent, and East Anglia's royal lineages. Scholars believe that when Woden lost his divine status as Anglo-Saxon paganism declined, he was adopted as an ancestor in numerous royal families. Some other important gods were Thunor and Tiw. The pre-Christian Anglo-

Saxons also believed in a range of supernatural beings like dragons, elves, and Nicor (shape-shifting water creatures).

Thunor is the second most popular deity in Anglo-Saxon paganism. The hammer and the swastika were believed to be this god's symbols representing thunderbolts. These symbols were found in many Anglo-Saxon graves and carved on excavated cremation urns. Place names related to Thunor include Thundersley or Thunder's Woods in Wessex, Thunderfield in Surrey, and Thunores hlaew or Thunor's Mound in Kent. The third important divine figure in Anglo-Saxon paganism is Tiw, who is identified with the Polaris star, and sometimes is referred to as the god of war.

The most popular female divinity among the pantheon of Anglo-Saxon pagan gods was Frig though there is very little evidence of how and in what role she was worshipped. Some scholars suggest that she might have been the goddess of love and/or festivity. Scholars also believe that her name is associated with place names such as Frethern in Gloucestershire, and Froyle, Freefolk, and Frobury in Hampshire.

Followers of the Anglo-Saxon pagan belief system demonstrated their devotion for their gods and goddesses in various ways, especially by sacrificial rituals, which included sacrificing animals as well as inanimate objects. These special rituals were performed at important religious festivals in temples, evidence of which is seen even today.

Scholars believe that it is likely that most of the cult practices and rituals took place in the outdoors. There is little evidence regarding the afterlife beliefs of Anglo-Saxon pagans, although excavated tombs reveal that the dead were buried or cremated with grave goods. Today, we know of nearly 1200 Anglo-Saxon pagan cemeteries. Both burials and cremations were used in funeral practices. The cremated remains were collected in urns and buried along with grave goods.

Men appear to have been buried with at least one weapon, usually a seax (an Old English word for knife). But some graves revealed more than one weapon, including spears, shields, and swords. Interestingly, non-human animal body parts such as sheep, goats and oxen, were also found, indicating that the funeral customs could have included meats to be buried to serve as food for the deceased on his or her journey to the afterlife.

Anglo-Saxon legends, myths, and other works of literature were transmitted orally, and there is very little evidence of written sources. The only extant Anglo-Saxon epic is the tale of Beowulf. Even scholars regard this surviving text as being recorded by Sepa, a Christian monk. The period when he might have written it is unclear, and most historians believe it could have been written anytime between the 8th and 11th centuries.

Beowulf's story is set in Scandinavia and is based around Beowulf, a Geatish warrior who journeys to Denmark to kill a monster named Grendel. Geats, also referred to as Goths, occupied Gotaland or Geatland (present-day southern Sweden). Beowulf defeats Grendel, who was wreaking havoc on the Hrothgar kingdom and his equally dangerous mother.

According to the story, after the successful slaying of Grendel and his mother, Beowulf becomes the king of Gotaland. He dies when trying to fight off a ferocious dragon. We know this poem has its origins in Anglo-Saxon paganism because of the various pagan beliefs elaborated on within the text, including cremation beliefs. Still, it contains references to biblical figures, which makes it look like the work of a clergyman.

Modern Paganism has adopted various elements of pre-Christian Anglo-Saxon practices, especially in the modern religious movements such as Heathenry and Wicca. Wicca, particularly the Seax-Wicca sect, combines Wiccan and Anglo-Saxon beliefs and deity names.

Chapter 3: Heathenry Vs. Asatru

Heathenry is a new religious movement that is known by multiple other terms, including Heathenism, Germanic Neopaganism, or contemporary Germanic Paganism. It was developed in Europe in the early 20th century and is based on pre-Christian beliefs followed by the Germanic tribes from the Iron Age until the Early Middle Ages.

Heathenry is an attempt to revive and reconstruct ancient belief systems using remaining evidence from folklore, history, and archeology. Heathenry is a polytheistic belief system that focuses on a pantheon of gods, goddesses, and deities from the pre-Christian era of the Germanic regions. The followers of this new religious movement have adopted the cosmological perspectives from ancient societies and tribes. They believe in animism too, or that the cosmos, including the natural world we see around us, are filled with spirits and other divine beings and creatures.

"Heathens," as the followers of Heathenry call themselves, believe in a system of ethics based on loyalty, personal integrity, and honor. Beliefs in the afterlife are varied but this topic does not get much attention among the Heathens.

Practitioners are trying to understand and revive forgotten belief systems by using one or more of the following sources:

- Old Norse texts related to Iceland, including the *Poetic Edda* and *Prose Edda*.

- Old English recordings such as Beowulf.

- German texts of the Middle Ages such as *Nibelungenlied*.

- Archeological evidence that throws light on the pre-Christian age of northern Europe.

- Folklore-based stories and tales collectively referred to as "Lore" by Heathens.

Heathenry believers perform sacrificial rites and rituals referred to as "blots," where a variety of libations and food are offered to their deities. Most of the rituals include a ceremony called symbel, which consists of offering a toast of an alcoholic beverage to the gods. Some practitioners also perform rituals to achieve an altered state of reality through visions and wisdom from the invisible spiritual beings and deities. The most popular of these rituals include the seiðr and galdr.

While some practitioners indulge in these rituals individually, some Heathens perform the ceremonies in little groups called "kindreds" or "hearths." The group rituals are usually conducted in open spaces or in buildings constructed specifically for this purpose.

The Origins and History of Heathenry

Heathenry is a new religious movement (NRM) or a Reconstructionist form of modern Paganism. This movement was developed to revive and get a contemporary understanding of the practices and rituals followed by the pre-Christian traditions and cultures of northern Europe, more specifically, the Germanic cultures.

Heathenry developed during the Romantic era of the 19th and early 20th centuries. During this period, pre-Christian tribes and societies of Germanic Europe gained a lot of popularity. Groups of believers actively worshipped and venerated deities of these ancient tribes of Austria and Germany in the 1900s and 1910s. Nearly all the newly formed belief systems dissolved after World War II.

In the 1970s, new formalized groups and organizations were established and developed in North America and Europe. The issue of race was a central theme in these organizations. The older sects adopted an attitude of racism, referred to as "folkish." These older divisions of Heathenry believed themselves to have ethnic links to a Germanic race, reserved only for white people, and more specifically, only for those with North European roots.

These small divisions within Heathenry combined the belief of racism with right-wing and white supremacist beliefs and perspectives. On the other hand, numerous Heathens had a Universalist approach proclaiming that their religion was open to all and was independent of origin, race, and other discriminatory elements.

The term Heathenry is often used to describe the new religious movement entirely. But there are many groups and sects within this movement, and each of these divisions has its own preferred name, which is based on its ideologies and belief systems. Heathens who believe and follow the Scandinavian sources and belief systems use the terms Ásatrú, Vanatrú, or Forn Sed. Other sects use the following terms/phrases:

- Anglo-Saxon traditions – Theodism or Fyrnsidu.

- German traditions – Irminism.

- Far-right and "folkish" perspectives – Odinism, Folkism, Wodenism, Wotanism, or Odalism.

It is currently believed that there are about 20,000 Heathens globally, with the most active practitioners living in America, Europe, and Australasia. Each of these groups interprets historical sources differently. Some are involved in reconstructing past practices and beliefs accurately.

Some others are open to experimentation and are willing to embrace new interpretations and innovations. And some other groups adopt practices and traditions including their own experiences and personal lessons gained by the experimentations. A few other sects and divisions of Heathenry combine Germanic cultures with ancient surviving practices of other geographies, including Afro-American religions, Hinduism, Buddhism, Taoism, etc.

Understanding Asatru

Asatru is one of the sects of Heathenism. "Tru" literally means "faith" in the Icelandic language, and therefore, Asatru translates to Aesir's faith or belief. As you already know, Aesir were gods from one of the tribes of deities worshipped in Norse Paganism. Asatru practitioners are called Asatruar. The primary focus of Asatru is on the Nordic gods and goddesses of Scandinavia but Asatruars' worship other deity groups, including the Vanir, elves, dwarfs, and valkyries.

Another name for Asatru is Vanatru, or those who venerate the Vanir tribe of Nordic deities. A smaller group of Asatruars venerates and worships the jotnar (or jotunn) and refers to their community as Rokkatru. Forn Sed or the "Old Way" is another common term used to replace Asatru. Most of the right-wing people prefer to call their belief system Odinism, Wodenism, etc.

Understanding Heathenism and Asatru

As you already know by now, Paganism is a collective term including multiple forms of belief systems and traditions, including Celtic Paganism, Slavic Paganism, and even Wicca, and so forth. Heathenism is specifically for Germanic and Nordic gods and deities, including Odin, Thor, Grigg, Friya, and others.

Asatru is a modern Icelandic term that is related specifically to the worship and veneration of the Aesir gods. Asatru is a term that is used often in formal settings among the Asatru community, more often than Norse Paganism or Heathenism. Although followers of Asatru know and believe in the Vanir gods, they don't talk about or worship any other deities but those from the Aesir tribe. Some believe that Vanatru is a direct outcome of the lack of involvement and engagement by the Asatruar with the Vanir deities.

Asatru has a fairly rigid and formalized set of rules to follow. The things that are expected of you as a follower of that faith could lead to a large formal community that follows the belief system. On the other hand, Heathenism and Norse Paganism seek small-scale communities that are self-sufficient in each of their traditions, cultures, and belief systems.

Although the emergence of Heathenism and Asatru are rooted in Norse Paganism, many of the modern Asatruar tend to use the term Asatru because, for the uninitiated, words like Paganism, Norse Paganism, and Heathenism tend to have a negative connotation.

One of the most important things to know about Asatru is that there is no missionary or proselytizing events that happen. People can join the community if they want. There is nothing given in return for becoming a Heathen. You do it only if it is your calling.

The Asatru Association

The Asatru Association is an Icelandic religious formalized organization of Heathenry established on the First Day of Summer in 1972 by Sveinbjörn Beinteinsson, a farmer and poet. The First Day of Summer in Iceland is a national holiday and is celebrated on the first Thursday after April 18th annually. The Asatru Association was recognized and registered as a religious organization in 1973. The chief religious official or the highest office of the Asatru Association is referred to as "Allsherjargodi," an elected post.

The priests in Asatru are called Godi, and each Godi is given a congregation called godord to work with. While each godord is more or less connected to certain geographic regions, there is no compulsion to join any specific godord. You are free to join any congregation that you like.

The legal approval allowed the organization to conduct legally binding rituals and ceremonies as well as to collect a share of the church tax, which is imposed by the tax on religious congregations to run and manage churches and their employees. Sveinbjörn Beinteinsson led this organization from its inception in 1972 until his death in 1993. During his time, the membership of this organization did not exceed 100 people, and there was not much activity.

The second Allsherjargodi was Jörmundur Ingi Hansen, who led the organization from 1994 to 2002, and it was during this time when the Asatru Association witnessed considerable activity and growth. The third and current leader is the musician Hilmar Örn Hilmarsson, who took charge in 2003.

Asatru does not conform to a fixed religion, theology, or dogma. Each individual is free to have his or her own beliefs. For example, many Wiccan members are also members of the Asatru Association. The Asatru priests believe in a pantheistic perspective. The communal blot feast is the central ritual of Asatru. The priests also conduct naming ceremonies called gooar, weddings, funerals, coming of age, and other rituals too.

The Blot Ritual

The communal blot festival is an important occasion in Asatru. The blot starts with hallowing the ritual with a specific formula. Another important element at the start of the blot ritual is the declaration of truce and peace among all the members present there. The chanting of verses from the *Poetic Edda* follows this ceremony. The next stage consists of passing a drinking horn wherein the participants toast and drink in honor of the gods, ancestors, and wights. Libations are also offered to the worshipped deities.

This initial part of the ritual usually happens outdoors, followed by a communal feast that usually takes place indoors. The communal feast is accompanied by entertainment in various forms, including music and dance. There are four annual blot ceremonies, including:

- The Jolablot or the Yuleblot on Winter Solstice – a special event on this day is the lighting of candles by children to celebrate the Sun's rebirth.

- The Sigurblot or the Victory blot on the First Day of Summer.

- The Sumarblot or summer blot on Summer Solstice.

- The Veturnattablot or Winter Night blot on the First Day of Winter.

In addition to these four main blots, other forms of similar rituals for individuals such as gooar and even local blots for smaller communities are conducted. All the rituals and ceremonies of the Asatru Association, including the weekly meetings, are open to the public.

Asatru Perspectives

The modern Asatru/Heathenism community has three primary perspectives, namely, Universalism, Folkism, and Tribalism. Of these three, the first two perspectives are the main ones, while the third, Tribalism, takes a middle-ground approach.

Universalism - According to the people who believe in this perspective, anyone from any background can become a Heathen. A Universalist perspective offers more freedom of choice to everyone, even while giving greater options for Heathenism to grow and expand its reach across the globe.

Therefore, a Universalist will welcome a Japanese person into his or her fold of Asatru as long as the initiate is willing to understand the lore of Norse Paganism, live his or her life based on the nine virtues, learn and understand the runes of Asatru, and take responsibility for his or her own actions. Most importantly, a Universalist values common sense.

One of the primary arguments against Universalism, especially from the Tribalists and Folkish, is that it is very open-ended. People of the other two perspectives believe that there should be a few vital threshold criteria that need to be met before allowing anyone to practice Asatru. Conversely, Universalists believe that these vital criteria are already there, those which have been discussed in the previous paragraph.

Folkism - The Folkish perspective believes that Asatru is an ethnic religion and entry should be restricted only to those with a North European heritage. This belief of Folkism is based on the idea that ethnic religions connect followers to the local landscape, bloodline, ancestors, and traditions. So, outsiders can't find a connection with the ethnic elements and will fail to be genuine practitioners.

Many people accuse those who follow Folkism of being white supremacists because of their rigid approach regarding their entry into Asatru, but the Folkish argue that their stand has nothing to do with white supremacy but is based on the deep belief that every ethnic community must worship its own ancestors.

People who oppose Folkism also use another argument in their favor. They quote the presence of multiple non-Norse people and characters in the Eddas and other Norse folklore and legends. These non-Norse characters took part in rituals and rites too. Also, slaves in the Nordic community came from other lands and regions, including Slavic, Celtic, and even Middle Eastern. And many of these slaves were freed and emancipated by their masters and allowed to settle and live the Nordic life.

On the other hand, the Norse people who migrated to other lands also adopted and absorbed those lands' cultures and traditions. Despite these arguments, Folkism stands firm in its principle to not allow all and sundry into the Asatru fold.

Tribalism – Folkism and Universalism are at the two ends of the Asatru spectrum, while those who follow Tribalism take a middle stand. They accept and embrace the Folkish stand of the need for a deep connection and feeling for Norse culture to be able to call oneself an Asatru. Surface-level adoption of Asatru principles is not enough. A person can be inducted into the clan in one of two ways, specifically if he or she is of Germanic origin or if the person is converted, adopted or takes an oath into the community.

Regardless of the perspective you choose to take, the vital thing is to remember that the Nordic people greatly valued courage, honor, freedom, individuality, growth, and development. Also, those of us who feel a calling to join the path of Asatru will have to experience the belief system only in the current, modern-day scenario. Therefore, being able to practice the Old Norse religion, the way it existed during the Viking Age, is impossible.

The critical thing is that your connection to Asatru must be deep. It calls for a commitment and it should definitely go beyond learning about Odin, Thor, and other deities. Wearing a miniature of Thor's hammer around your neck is not enough. You will have to learn to live the life of a true Norse pagan.

Chapter 4: The Nine Noble Virtues and Other Codes

Now that you have a fairly good idea of the meaning and context of Norse Paganism, Heathenry, and Asatru, it is time to get deeper into what defines the life of an Astruar. A few types of frameworks of codes and value systems govern Asatru. These codes act as guidelines for the followers to lead a life based on Asatru principles. These codes were formed and collated from various sources, including the Icelandic Sagas and the *Poetic Edda*.

The Nine Noble Virtues, also referred to as NNV or 9NV, consist of two sets of ethical and moral situational guidelines. Sir John Yeowell and John Gibbs-Bailey created one set of codes. Sir Yeowell, also known as Stubba, and John Gibbs-Bailey, also known as Hokuld, were members of the Odinic Rite, an international organization dedicated to Odinism and Asatru.

Some believers credit Edred Thorsson with codifying the first set of NNV when he was a member of the Asatru Folk Assembly (AFA). Stephen A. McNallen, a member of the AFA, codified the second set of the NNV. Edred Thorsson and Darban-i-Den were the pen names of Stephen Edred Flowers. Some other sets of Asatru moral and ethical codes include:

- The Nine Charges – discussed in detail in another section of this chapter.

- The Six-Fold Goal – right wisdom, harvest, might, firth, and love.

- The Aesirian Code of Nine – knowledge, honor, protect, change, flourish, conflict, fairness, balance, and control.

The Nine Noble Virtues

Courage

The Asatru defines courage as an element of pagan virtue that drives an individual to act and behave in the right way, even in the absence of reward or in the face of certain defeat. This definition clearly emerged in all the Norse stories and legends. The powerful monsters are central to all Norse mythological themes, but they were not given an honorable character.

Contrarily, the heroes found potent solutions to kill the monsters driven by sheer courage and willpower. In fact, the concept of courage being paramount in a person's life is the reason, however misplaced, that gave rise to the opinions that the Vikings were godless.

The Viking people were so focused on their courage to do the right thing that they believed that martial heroism was a power of its own. In today's world, courage is more than martial bravery. It also means to stand up for the right thing. For example, turning into a whistleblower when the company you work for has violated laws is considered to be a courageous thing to do, according to the Asatru.

Norse Paganism believed that courage was all about having faith and trust in your own strength. Courage, according to Asatru, also includes being brave to live according to the Nine Noble Virtues. Asatruars believe that it is vital to stand up in a hostile world to be counted among the true and authentic people of character.

Courage is:

- Having the conviction and inner strength to face the enormity of the task at hand.

- Standing by your friends and family.

- Keeping alive and following Asatru principles.

From the *Poetic Edda,* Havamal explains courage like this, "The coward believes that he will live forever, if he holds back in the battle, but in old age he shall have no peace, though spears have spared his limbs."

Truth

The truth is to say and do what is right and true. It is the willingness to be straightforward and honest. If you cannot be honest, it is better not to say anything at all. And in the same way, if you have to talk, then it is vital that you speak the truth as you see it and not as what others want to hear. Telling the truth might be painful at times, but it is better to deal with the short-term effects of pain by being truthful rather than lying, which has far more harmful consequences.

Courage and truth are interlinked, because courage fosters and encourages truth, and the reverse is also true. When you build your ability to speak the truth in your life, you also build the courage to face the consequences. Truth is the underlying virtue of holiness, even as it strengthens us toward being courageous. In the absence of truthfulness in your character, you are unlikely to meet with any kind of spiritual realization.

Being courageous and truthful requires persistent efforts. You must incessantly strive to do the right thing and live according to what you know and believe as being true and correct. Truthfulness is a virtue valued by our ancestors. Being truthful also helps you in being modest. You find it easy not to exaggerate your achievements as well as accept your failures with humility.

There is an interesting warning with regard to speaking the truth. Undoubtedly, you must always try to speak the truth, but you must not be naïve enough to talk the truth with people who spout lies to you. According to the Havamal, it might be a good thing to counter lies with lies to guarantee that you are not taken for a ride by the scamsters of the world.

One of the verses about truth explained in Havamal goes as follows, "Do not promise something you cannot live up to. Breaking your word has serious consequences."

Honor

Honor is all about the value of recognizing and accepting nobility, both within and outside of us. Honor is not only your own feeling of self-worth rooted in your noble character, but also showing respect to others. Perhaps honor is one of the most difficult virtues to define because different people can interpret it differently.

The importance of living an honorable life is contained in this small proverb in the *Poetic Edda,* "Everything and everyone in this world dies. However, the reputation of dead people never dies." So, good or bad deeds survive even after our deaths, and they carry the glory or burden of our soul.

Astruars see honor as the value they add to the community. The answers to the following questions can tell you whether honor exists in your personality:

- Are you an upstanding person in your community?

- Do people come to you for help and advice, especially regarding morals and principles?

- Do people trust your word? Or do they always second-guess what you say?

Without honor, we cannot evolve or progress in our lives. Also, dishonorable people tend to hold back the progress of their families and community. Our actions and deeds reflect our honor and our self-worth. Striving to be worthy of the place we occupy in the world, community, and family is all part of an honorable life.

Fidelity

Fidelity is the willingness to be loyal to your faith and belief systems, including the deities, and to your community, friends, and yourself. There are many levels of loyalty, which are individual-specific and situational-specific. Each of us knows and understands the depth of the various levels of loyalty we feel within ourselves.

Fidelity in Asatru includes your commitment:

- To your faith (Asatru).
- To your community and kindred.
- To your family responsibilities.
- To your intention of making the world a better place.

Courage forms the foundation on which loyalty and commitment build their strengths. When we are courageous, we find the power to hold the bonds that tie us to our faith, community, and family. These bonds of togetherness drive us to accept ourselves as a conduit through which progress for the family and community takes place. These bonds of commitment are what weave the tapestry of Asatru.

Interestingly, "troth" is the German word for loyalty and faith. In ancient times, a warrior who survived while his lord died—or failed to die for his tribe or community's safety and protection—was dishonored and shunned by his society.

Fidelity is also about honoring your promises and oaths, including wedding vows. Oaths and promises are sacred contracts, and those who break these contracts are the biggest offenders, according to Asatru NNV.

Generosity and fidelity are connected to each other at a very deep level. Giving is a way to strengthen fidelity. When you are loyal, then you find your ability to be generous and giving also improves. Giving is not only in the form of materialistic things but also in the gift of love, time, etc. Importantly, the act of generosity is not one-sided but has to work both ways. According to ancient Heathens, if you do not return the giver with your own generosity, then you will lose the power of the gift you received.

A passage in Havamal on fidelity goes like this, "If you have a friend you trust, then it is your duty to pray for his goodwill, to exchange gifts and thoughts, and visit his house even as you invite him to your house as often as possible."

Discipline

Discipline, or self-discipline, is your ability to be hard on yourself to improve your life. Once you are disciplined, then you should try to help others in need toward their self-development. As the concept of discipline and self-development spreads in the community, the entire tribe or clan progresses and great purposes are achieved.

The lesson of discipline should not be taught through words, but through actions. It is easy to tell others to do what you say and not do what you do. Even so, Asatru does not approve of this approach. You will have to lead by example. It calls for an enormous amount of willpower and discipline to stay on the difficult path of Asatru instead of choosing another potentially easier path. Only when you stay on your path of commitment will others follow suit.

Discipline and fidelity work in tandem. Discipline provides the willpower to be loyal, and fidelity, in turn, motivates you to be disciplined and be true and committed to your values and principles. These two virtues help us shape our worth and destiny. Havamal describes discipline in the following way, "A person who rises early, keeps few slaves, does his own work rises in his life and earns wealth and prosperity. A person who sleeps late loses a lot in his life."

Hospitality

Hospitality is the sense of service you have. It reflects your willingness to share what you have with your people and community. Of course, this does not mean that you mindlessly give away everything you have to anyone who comes knocking at your door. Hospitality is about sharing and giving and has a reciprocity effect as well.

When guests come to your house, it is your duty to make them as comfortable as you can, and to offer them food and drink. Hospitality is a very important virtue in Asatru: their gods travel all over the cosmos, including to Midgard or the realm of human beings. With that in mind, a guest in your house could be a god in disguise, and it is your duty to honor him or her.

Also, hospitality drives a sense of readiness to help and assist people in need. It drives interdependence in the community and forges strong bonds among the members. In fact, for ancestors, hospitality was not just a virtue, it was a necessity. In those days, traveling long distances posed a lot of difficulties and was also dangerous. Yet, traveling was important for trade and commerce. So, Norsemen and women of those times freely opened their homes not only to their friends and other known tribespeople but also to strangers.

People who came knocking would be provided with a warm place to rest their tired feet, warm food to fill their bellies, and even warm clothes to wear. In return, the guest was expected to eat moderately, entertain their hosts with songs and stories, and give little gifts such as small trinkets. Havamal talks about the importance of hospitality in the following way: "A guest who has traveled needs the warmth of a fire for his numb knees, warm water to wash, clean clothes and food to fend off the hunger and cold."

Self-Reliance

This virtue reflects your spirit of independence. When you are self-reliant, you are independent for yourself and empower your family toward this virtue. It is important to remember that being self-reliant does not mean you should deny your interconnectedness with others. It is about having the ability to first take care of yourself, and then work toward helping others in need. Self-reliance helps you to provide food to eat for yourself as well as share what you have with others in need.

Self-reliance teaches you to find solutions for your problems. It teaches you to build skills to make your life better than it is today. It teaches you not to waste time and to use your skills effectively to learn new things so that you can bring prosperity to your life.

Self-reliance is a vital element of freedom. When you are self-reliant, you are free to make your own decisions. You can think for yourself and find solutions that suit you best. When you taste freedom, you earn more freedom, and you become increasingly self-reliant. Self-reliance is about using your own wisdom and intellect to understand yourself and the world around you.

Industriousness

This virtue is all about your willingness to work hard at all times and to strive for efficiency. The trick is in seeing the journey of industriousness as a joyous activity. It is imperative that we work hard to achieve our goals, to find what we seek. Without hard work and perseverance, we can never reach our goals.

And yet, working hard without time to relax and enjoy your life is also not the Asatru way. Industriousness is a virtue that has hard work at its core, but it also means you take pride in your work. Asatru's definition of industriousness goes a little above and beyond too. The value system of Asatru says this about industriousness: "Unless you are disabled, a full-time student, or already employed, it is your duty to find a job and do it diligently."

If you have a problem finding a job, then endeavor to find some like-minded people and start a venture. Asatruars believe that without work, there can be no self-worth. We cannot provide for our families. We cannot achieve our goals or strive to reach perfection in our lives. Being lazy is one of the worst lessons you can teach your children.

Industriousness also means striving hard for self-improvement. We should not be happy with mediocrity or working in a way that simply helps us to survive. Our industriousness should drive us to achieve greater efficiency and productivity and to thrive in our lives. This virtue is specifically useful in the modern era where life has become very convenient. It is easy to go to a grocery store, come home, put some ingredients together, and create a meal for yourself, unlike the ancient times when there was a lot of work to do, such as cows to milk, fields to till, cattle to feed, and much more, before food was ready to be eaten. Thus, industriousness was a necessity to prevent starvation.

Today, laziness may not result in starvation, but it does cause a lot of other problems, including joblessness and a total loss of self-worth, without which your life can be a living hell. Self-reliance and industriousness work hand in hand. Your sense of independence will drive you to do your work without depending on anyone. This approach drives you to work hard. You don't wait for things to be done by others, and you don't wait for your life to be handed over to you on a platter.

Perseverance

Perseverance is a virtue that empowers one to stand up and try again despite repeated failures. It is your ability to return stronger after every setback you encounter. It is your ability to stay on the path of your life's purpose until you achieve it. Perseverance is about not giving up until you succeed. Hard work and perseverance are essential elements for success. As an Asatruar, it is your duty to persevere because perseverance is vital for survival. It is a dynamic part of nature. If we don't persevere, we will stagnate and die.

These Nine Noble Virtues form the structural framework of the Asatru community. The members are encouraged to remember and implement each of these ethics so that they can lead a fulfilling, meaningful life, even as they bring happiness to their families and community.

The Nine Charges

The Odinic Rite established the Nine Charges in the 1970s. These nine codes of Asatru ethics and morals are as follows:

1. To maintain honesty and loyalty to a trusted friend; even if he or she hits me, I will not strike back.

2. Never make false promises because the outcome of broken promises is huge and grim.

3. To be gentle with the poor and humble.

4. To respect the elderly and the wise.

5. To fight against all evils and foes of the faith, family, and community.

6. To return friendliness but not to give in to the promise of an untried and untested stranger.

7. Not to give in to the foolish words of a drunken man.

8. To respect and listen to the wise words of our ancestors.

9. To abide by the rules set by lawful authority.

Chapter 5: The Aesir, Vanir, and Jotnar

This chapter is dedicated to the pantheon of Norse gods, goddesses, and other divine beings. Many of the Asatruars seek guidance and help from these deities, but it is important to know that not all practitioners worship or pray to the gods. Instead, followers may seek clarity and guidance to solve problems and lead a meaningful, fulfilling life.

Creation Myth of Norse Mythology

According to Norse Paganism, before the start of time, there was a bottomless abyss referred to as Ginnungagap. This abyss separated the fiery land of Muspelheim and the icy lands of Niflheim. The two realms became powerful and strong and clashed against each other. The fire from Muspelheim thawed the ice in Niflheim and turned it to water drops, which held the potential for life.

The first living being, according to Norse Mythology, was Ymir. Ymir was a hermaphrodite giant who was created from the life-giving water drops. Ymir created children from his armpits as well as rubbed his two legs together, which gave rise to the jotnar, giant, and many other races. Although all the races were born of the same parent, a lot of animosities grew among races, and after a few generations, there was continuous discord among them.

Ymir's descendants were Odin, Vili, and Ve, who together killed Ymir. Then they used Ymir's bones, blood, teeth, eyelashes, hair, skull, and brain to create the Nordic world. The dome of Ymir's skull became the sky that arched over the earth. His blood became the waters of the lakes, rivers, and seas. His brain became clouds. His bones were transformed into hills and mountains, and his hair became trees.

The gods then created a protective fence out of Ymir's eyelashes to separate Jotunheimer, the giant's realm, from what was going to become the Midgard or the human realm. The gods then took over the job of overseeing this border they created to provide safety to the human world.

Norse gods are primarily divided into two categories, the Aesir and Vanir.

The Aesir and Vanir

The Vanir – Historically, the Vanir, a tribe of farmers (worshipped later as ancient powerful gods), are believed to have come to Scandinavia and other parts of northern Europe about 5000 years ago. They brought the gift and power of agriculture, which is why they are considered farmer gods and goddesses. They came to this area after the flooding of the Black Sea.

Considering they were farmers, the Vanir gods are known for their connection to fertility. The important Vanir gods are Njord, Freya, and Freyr. Other deities include the Earth, Night, Day, Sun, and Moon. Day was believed to be the child of Night. Sun was female, and Moon was male.

The Aesir – Historically, the Aesir could have been male warriors who rode on horses and chariots. They are believed to have come from the East during the Indo-European invasions, which took place more than 1000 years after the entry of the Vanir. The Aesir warriors are believed to have wiped out most of the farmers or Vanirs (who were already living in Scandinavia); they retained the culture of the Vanirs and merged it with their own.

The most important Aesir gods were Odin, Frigg, Thor, and Tyr. According to Norse Paganism, half the warriors that die in battle are taken to Valhalla, a great hall in Asgard where Odin rules. The remaining slain warriors are taken to Folkvang (by Freya, the Vanir god), which is ruled by the Valkyries. The Vanirs and Aesirs are believed to have coexisted because the two groups, despite their antagonism, were required to combine their powers in order to prosper.

Norse Deities

Let us look at some gods and goddesses of Norse mythology and how they interacted with each other and with human beings too.

Odin

Odin was the supreme deity in Norse Mythology. He was the greatest and the most revered immortal among Norse gods and was the father of the Aesir tribe. Odin was an awe-inspiring figure who ruled over Asgard. He was not only the god of war but also the god of poetry and magic. His famous possessions are his horse Sleipnir, and his ring, Draupnir.

He is known by many other names, including Wotan and Wodan or Woden. Odin translates to "Master of Fury." He is also the most mysterious and complex god in the pantheon of Norse gods and goddesses.

But above all, Odin's primary trait was an unrelenting quest for knowledge and wisdom. His search for wisdom was not peaceful or serene, but one of continuous activity. His might is compared to the power of a relentless storm, which is never still until it completes its phase of destruction. In the same way, Odin's search for wisdom and knowledge is filled with activities and adventures.

He had two wolves, two ravens, and the Valkyries to help him in his quest. His quest for knowledge was so deep that he willingly sacrificed one of his eyes so that he could see the cosmos more clearly than before. Also, he hung from the World Tree or Yggdrasil for nine days and nights. This perseverance brought him the knowledge of the runic alphabet. He sought knowledge relentlessly, and this attitude helped him to unlock many of the secrets and mysteries of the cosmos.

Interestingly, Odin was not pure at heart, even if he was a god or the king of gods. He is often portrayed as being punished for unfairness and not respecting law and convention. Odin was the god of rulers as well as outlaws. Adam of Bremen, an 11th-century historian, describes Odin's character excellently in the following words: "When Odin was among friends, he made everyone happy with his magic and poetry. When he was at war, the enemies would run helter-skelter at this terrifyingly grim demeanor."

Frigg and Freya

Frigg was Odin's wife and the mighty queen of Asgard. She was the only goddess who had the power and position to sit next to her husband. She was a paragon of love, beauty, fate, and fertility. This powerful Norse goddess had the power of divination, but a blanket of secrecy surrounded her.

Despite her powerful position among the Norse gods, Frigg gets very little mention in the surviving sources of Norse mythology. Her characteristics appear to be combined with those of Freya, the goddess from the Vanir tribes, which, perhaps, reflects the mutual evolution of a friendship between the two tribes.

Freya is such a pleasure seeker that she is considered equivalent to the modern "party girl." In fact, Loki accuses her of sleeping with all the gods, elves, dwarfs, and her own brother too. Despite that, she was much more than just a pleasure-seeker. A highly protective mother, she coerced an oath from all the elements of nature, beasts, poisons, and weapons that they will not harm or kill Balder, her loving and brilliant son.

Freya was a passionate and sensual Norse goddess who was associated with beauty, love, and fertility, similar qualities connected to Frigg. Both Frigg and Freya are depicted as a volva, a female magician of Norse Paganism. They work with a particular form of magic called seidr, which involves deciding destinies as well as bringing about positive changes in the system. Both Frigg and Freya used falcon feathers to shapeshift into the bird.

Freya is deeply connected with seidr, a form of magic and shamanism that works to bring about positive changes in the world and cosmos. The power of seidr is spoken of in glowing terms in Norse mythology. With the magic of seidr in her hand, a powerful magician like Freya could weave new events and personal experiences into a being.

In the Viking age, a volva was deemed to be a sorceress who traveled from place to place to perform seidr magic on commission. She would be compensated for her magic work with food, clothing, and accommodation. A volva was looked upon with a mixture of awe, fear, longing, and idolization.

Balder

Balder was the son of Odin and Frigg. In Norse Mythology, Balder is described as living between heaven and Earth. He was handsome, radiant, kind, and a fair god. Although he was an immortal god, he was killed by deceit with mistletoe, an element that contained his life as well as his death.

Balder was loved by all gods, goddesses, and the jotnar because of his great looks and cheerful and gracious nature. When Balder began to have dreams about his death, Frigg went around to all the elements and beings in the cosmos and secured oaths from all of them not to hurt or kill Balder.

Once this was done, the gods amused themselves by throwing things at him and seeing him unhurt by anything. His mother made one small mistake. She left out the mistletoe from her oath list because she thought it was too small to cause any harm to her son. Loki knew about this, and with the intention of creating harmless mischief, he gave Hod (or Hodr, the blind god) a sprig of mistletoe and asked him to throw it at Balder, as the other gods were doing. When this small mistletoe touched Balder's body, he fell dead.

Loki

This mischievous god was a shapeshifter too. He could transform into many animal forms. Traditionally, Loki is described as being a wight of fire. The fire elements are represented in the description of his traits as an indispensable companion, a deadly master, and an untrustworthy servant. Loki was a tricky god, capable of creating a lot of mischief.

The gifts that Loki could confer on people are believed to be speech, hearing, sight, and appearance. Loki is shown as indulging in double-agent behavior, often betraying one side in favor of another. He creates trouble for the gods and goddesses and finds it delightful to play pranks, including malicious ones. So, while he is known to bring trouble to the gods, he has also been known to rescue them in times of need. Loki is the one who brought the gods many of their famous possessions, including Odin's horse Sleipnir and his ring Draupnir and Thor's hammer, Mjolnir.

As previously mentioned, Loki placed a branch of mistletoe in the hands of Hod, a blind god, and fooled him into throwing it at Balder, instantly killing the son of Frigg and Odin.

Thor

Thor was the most popular and famous son of Odin, and his mother was Earth. He was the protector of the human race and realm. He was also the god of thunder and wielded a powerful hammer called Mjolnir. Thor was famous for his strength, bravery, righteousness, and great healing powers. Another name of Thor is Thunar.

He inherited the powers of storm, wind, and air from his father, Odin. Thor was a warrior god par excellence. He was the ideal god that every human warrior strived hard to emulate. He is the invincible protector of the Aesir clan, as well as their realm, Asgard. His courage and sense of commitment and duty were unparalleled and unshakeable. His strength doubles when he wears his special belt, called Megingjard, which was a gift from his mother.

Thor's most famous weapon is his hammer, the Mjolnir, and he goes nowhere without it. For the Asatruars, Thor embodies thunder, and his hammer embodies lightning. Thor's biggest rival is Jormungand, the great serpent that lies curled around the Earth. In Ragnarok, Thor is believed to die at the hands of this great snake. Thor's wife was Sif, whose famous golden hair made her the protector of yellow ready-to-harvest cornfields.

Freyr

Freyr was an important Vanir clan god who was respected and revered highly. He was the god of prosperity and controlled the weather conditions. Freyr was often depicted with a phallus. Freyr is worshipped as the "foremost of the gods." No one hated him, thanks to his ability to confer wealth and prosperity on people who made him happy.

He is often represented as ecological and sexual prowess, including the health and wellbeing of an individual, peace, wealth, bountiful harvests, etc. In addition to his erect, enormous phallus, Freyr is also depicted with his boar, Gullinborsti, translated to the "one with the golden bristles."

Heimdall

Heimdall was famous for his "white skin" and was considered to be the "shiniest" of all the Norse deities. He was one of Odin's sons. He protected Asgard against attacks and invasions and sat on top of Bifrost, a divine rainbow bridge that connected Midgard, the human realm, to Asgard, the realm of the gods.

Heimdall's home is called Himinbjorg or the Sky Cliffs, on top of the Bifrost. He hardly needs sleep and therefore, is the best guard for Asgard. His eyesight is so sharp that he can see things within hundreds of miles, both during the day and by night. His hearing is so powerful that he can hear wool growing on a sheep's body and the grass growing out of the ground. His horn, Gjallarhorn or Resounding Horn, raises the alarm when he sees danger approaching Asgard.

Hel

Hel was a Norse goddess who ruled over the Norse underworld, Helheim, which was also referred to as Hel. Appearing death-like with pale skin, she nurtured and accommodated anyone who entered her realm. The meaning of her name and her realm is "hidden."

Hel was the daughter of Loki and Angrboda, a giantess. This goddess is depicted as being harsh, cruel, and greedy. At her best, she is indifferent to both the living and the dead. Her most significant appearance in Norse mythology is when Balder dies. Hermod was sent as an emissary to Hel to try to persuade the goddess to return Balder because every living being was crying at his death. But Hel refused to give up Balder easily.

She placed a very harsh condition for his return. She said that if every last element in the cosmos shed a tear for Balder, then she would release him back to the land of the living. Hermod and the other gods got together and made sure every little item in the cosmos cried for Balder, except one giantess. For that one refusal to cry, Hel's terms were not met, and she didn't return Balder, and he remained dead.

Vidar

Vidar was the son of Odin and a giantess, Grid. His powers were equal to that of Thor. Though, he makes an appearance in only one place in Ragnarok. Vidar translates to "the wide-ruling one." Vidar was believed to have survived the cataclysmic end of the world, Ragnarok. Vidar survived the end of the world, thanks to a pair of shoes especially crafted for the event.

These magical shoes were made with magical powers. Vidar was able to beat Wolf Fenrir (the one who killed Odin) and not only avenge his father's death but also end the rampage of the evil animal. Although he is as powerful as Thor, he is known as a silent god, and nothing more other than his encounters at Ragnarok are mentioned in the various Norse mythological tales.

Vale

Another son of Odin, Vale (sometimes spelled as Vali) avenged the death of his brother, Balder, by killing the blind god, Hod, who had killed Balder with mistletoe, although under false pretenses given by Loki. His mother was the giantess Rindr. Vale is another survivor of Ragnarok.

Jotnar

Jotnar is the plural of jotunn, a Norse word for a type of divine being distinct from Norse gods and goddesses. Jotnar are defined with different terms and phrases, including thurs, risi, and troll. The term giant is often used as a synonym for jotunn. Yet, jotnar are not necessarily gigantic in size and form. Jotnar can range from alarmingly grotesque to exceedingly beautiful beings. Odin is believed to be a descendant of the jotnar, while other Norse deities such as Geror and Skadi are described as being jotnar.

The gods came later in the Norse creation myth. The jotnar were one of the first beings produced through the hermaphroditic powers of Ymir. They grew from sexless reproduction from certain parts of Ymir's body. The different beings from Ymir's sexless production intermingled with each other and also with the first god, Buri, who appeared in the cosmos. Buri married a jotunn named Bestla.

The jotnar are believed to have survived Ymir's death by sailing to safety through the flood caused by Ymir's blood. The jotnar are believed to reside in Jotunheimen. Negative connotations about the jotnar were rooted in the later versions of Scandinavian folklore. There is hardly a Norse tale without the presence of a jotunn, and the jotnar are presented as one of the prime antagonists, but they were also spouses, friends, parents, and grandparents of the Aesir and Vanir deities.

Loki – Loki was the most famous jotunn. He was the son of Farbauti and Laufey of the jotnar race. Loki was adopted and accepted into the Aesir tribe of gods and became Thor's friend and companion. Even so, he was known as a duplicitous character that could be as mischievous and trouble causing as he was capable of doing a lot of good.

Skadi – The goddess of winter seasons, including its elements such as ice, snow, skiing, hunting, and archery, Skadi was the daughter of Pjazi, the storm god. She is mentioned in various Norse mythology texts, including the *Prose Edda*, the *Poetic Edda*, *Heimskringla*, and also in multiple skaldic poems. She argued and won reparations for her slain father in three different ways:

- She got Odin to place her father's eyes like two stars in the night sky.

- She wanted the gods to make her laugh, but no one was successful at this until Loki managed to make the giantess laugh out loud in happiness.

- She got the gods to agree to let her choose one of the gods to marry. Interestingly, she wanted to choose by looking at their feet. Her intention was to marry Balder, the god of beauty, and she put forth this condition thinking that it would be easy to simply choose him by looking at his beautiful feet. Surprisingly, she ended up choosing Njord, the god of the sea.

Another important being of the jotnar race is Pjazi, Skadi's father, who kidnapped the goddess Idunn, helped by Loki. Goddess Idunn is associated with apples because she was the keeper of a wooden box made of ash wood called Eski, in which she kept special apples. The Eski is used to keep treasured personal possessions. These apples were special because as the gods grew old, they would bite into one of the fruits and regain their youth again.

Loki is forced to kidnap Idunn by Pjazi. The two of them lure the goddess into the forest area, and there, Pjazi takes the shape of an eagle and flies away with Idunn. Then, during the battle with the Aesir gods for her retrieval, Pjazi is killed, for which Skadi makes the gods pay in three different ways, as discussed above. In another story, King Utkarda-Loki, the ruler of Jotunheimer, battles Thor. Another jotunn Hrungir battles Thor too in one of the fiercest battles of Norse mythology.

The jotnar are associated with the elemental forces and the natural world of human beings. The chaotic and destructive energies of nature were dangerous for our ancestors, and so, it is easy to understand why the beings representing these powers are portrayed as antagonists and villains. Even so, many realms of nature were useful for humankind, whose energies were represented as friendly jotnar. For example, Aegir was the giant of the sea and a friend of the gods. He is depicted as hosting grand banquets for his friends from the realm of gods.

Therefore, the jotnar, like all beings of the cosmos, were neither evil nor good in their entirety. They did their best to survive and thrive in their lives, as did the gods of the Aesir and Vanir clans.

Ragnarok

According to Norse mythology, Ragnarok is the cataclysmic destruction of the entire cosmos. For the Vikings and followers of Norse Paganism, Ragnarok was a prophecy of disaster set to happen at an unknown and unspecified time in the future. This concept had an impactful effect on how Vikings lead their lives.

Ragnarok translates to "Fate of the Gods." This event will take place whenever the Norns, the spinners of fate, decide. Ragnarok will be a period of Great Winter, with biting cold winds and snow hitting the cosmos from all directions. The Sun's warmth will not come through at all, and the Earth will be plunged into unprecedented winters, which will last for more than three times longer than the normal winters.

Humankind will have no food, and survival will be at stake. It will be a period of continuous warfare as survival instincts take hold, driving brothers against brothers. Yggdrasil, the World Tree, will tremble. The stars will disappear. Fenrir, the monstrous wolf, and Jormungand, the mighty serpent, will be free from their chains and wreak havoc in the cosmos.

The gods will arm themselves and go to battle, despite knowing the horrible outcome of Ragnarok. The warriors who were preparing at Valhalla will join the battle and fight valiantly, but to no avail. After a slew of destructive battles with all the gods and everything in the cosmos destroyed and killed, the remains of the world will sink into the sea, and nothing but a void will be left.

While some believe this is the end of the tale, others believe that life will arise from this void, and a new and beautiful world will be created.

Even today, the richness and power of Norse mythology continues to haunt and mesmerize people across the globe, regardless of age, race, gender, etc. Replete with numerous sagas, reading and learning Norse mythology can unleash your imagination, transporting you to a world of excitement, adventure, and intrigue.

Chapter 6: Asatru and Nature

Nature is an important aspect of Asatru belief. Land spirits and nature spirits are inextricable elements of Asatru. This chapter is dedicated to this aspect of Norse Paganism.

Unraveling the Vaettir

The word vaettir comes from the Old Norse language and literally translates to "supernatural being." Vaettir, or wights, are nature spirits in Norse Paganism. Vaettir is primarily used to refer to a supernatural being such as landvaettir or land spirits. The word is also used to refer to any supernatural being in the cosmos, including the elves, dwarfs, and even the Aesir and Vanir gods.

Nature spirits are categorized into different families, the prominent ones being the Alfar (or elves) and the Dvergar (or dwarfs). The families often intermarried among themselves as well as with human beings.

Sjo vaettir (or sea spirits) and vatna vaettir (or water spirits) were the guardians and protectors of specific areas of water. For example, there would be a vatna vaettir for a lake or a river, and there would be a dedicated sjo vaettir for a sea or ocean.

Hus vaettir (or house spirits) were guardians of specific households. An example of a hus vaettir is the Swedish Tomte, a solitary nature spirit that guarded a farmstead. It was seen as benevolent and helpful most of the time. An illvatte, on the other hand, is a highly mischievous vaettir and can cause a lot of harm if it is angry or displeased.

Landvaettir (or land spirits) are protectors and guardians of specific grounds such as forest areas (referred to as skovaettir) and farms. When traveling and approaching an unknown land or forest area, Vikings were known to remove their headgear (usually made of carved dragon heads) so as not to frighten the land spirits and provoke them to attack the Vikings needlessly. In fact, the Vikings believed that they would incur bad luck from landvaettir.

Even today, the Icelandic people celebrate and show gratitude for the supernatural spirits who protect and safeguard their island. In fact, the Icelandic coat-of-arms has four land spirits designed on it. These four include a troll-eagle, a troll-bull, a handsome giant, and a dragon.

According to Norse mythology, troll-animals are the jotnar who have shapeshifted into the chosen animal's form and mental attitude. It is believed that these troll animals are very powerful and strong.

Wights in Scandinavian Folklore

According to Scandinavian folklore, wights are believed to look like ordinary human beings and live in underground societies. Like human beings, wights come in different shapes and sizes; they are beautiful and ugly, tall and short. Some sources of Scandinavian folklore highlight the ability of the wights to change shape and size, and even become invisible. They can transform themselves from little creatures to the size of human beings. They wear dresses similar to us too.

Just like humans, wights also take their cattle to graze. Some sources talk about bears being the pig-equivalent for wights, and elks are to them what oxen are to us. Wights usually live harmoniously in the human world, but they can hurt us or create problems for us if we do something they don't like, or if we hurt them or treat them badly.

Wights are guardians of the environment they live in. Wights living in forests are guardians of the forest, those living in and near lakes protect the waters and creatures of the lake, and those living in hills and mountains are guardians of the natural elements of that place. The wights will punish anyone infringing on these spaces.

Wights can also live under buildings and houses. If these places are not managed well, then usually the wights move away from that place. The punitive measures taken by wights against those who infringe, damage, or hurt them or their spaces include:

- Bad luck through animals.
- Diseases and other health issues.
- Causing poverty.

Sometimes, wights can take revenge by sucking on the fingers and toes of the children of the people who created disturbances until the children cry out in pain. The intensity of their punishments depends on the extent of damage and pain we give them, wittingly or otherwise. For example, if we destroy their homes, then they can do the same to our homes. They can set fire to our houses, destroy things, and even kill the people living in the houses.

In Iceland, it is common to consult a wight expert before building a house or even before building infrastructure such as roads and bridges. In fact, there are reports of unexplained road accidents in some parts of Sweden and Iceland, which are attributed to wights. For that reason, it is imperative that you follow certain rules and regulations when it comes to dealing with wights and their spaces. Some of these rules include:

• When walking on forest paths, it is important that you don't walk in the middle of the road because it is believed that the underground wights use this part of the path. Considering they are invisible to human beings, not following this rule of conduct can cause accidents and harm the wights, making them angry and vengeful. The wights tend to take revenge by destroying homes, buildings, tools, and other human elements of the people living in that area. They could also cause illness.

• Before you pour water outside, especially hot water, you should shout, "Watch out!" so that wights can move out of the way and not get drenched. If you don't do this, then the wights are likely to punish you with accidents or health problems.

• Anything that ends up on the floor or the ground belongs to the wights. So, it is vital that what has been dropped is not cleaned up immediately. You must give the wights time to take what they want and clean up only that which they have left behind.

If the wights are happy with your gifts, they reward you well. You could get prosperity, wealth, great partnerships, and relationships, and your health problems could also get solved. Sometimes, wights reward their well-wishers and those who keep them happy with gems and precious stones as well. Initially, the gift you receive may not look great, but it is important to take care of it because it could transform into something beautiful and invaluable overnight.

• The water that was used for bathing and cleaning young, unbaptized children should be disposed of with care. Old beliefs mention that this water should be thrown out only after hot coals are put in it. Also, the clothes of these children should not be hung outside to dry after sunset. If these rules are not followed correctly, then the wights could come and kidnap the children.

• You can contact wights and other supernatural beings if you wish, but you must not try to contact them for selfish reasons. You can do so to give them a gift or to simply stay in touch. Wights will decide if they want to help you only when they see how truly unselfish you are. Remember that wights don't know or care about your needs and desires. They don't like being treated like servants too. They will help you only when they want to, and they know and believe you deserve their help.

When you are trying to contact the wights, choose a time when the sunlight is not too bright or where electric lights are not too glaring. Wights don't like bright sunlight or electric light. Also, remember not to leave any trash behind.

There are multiple stories about wights causing harm to human beings, including picking up children in anger or taking revenge. Wights are also known for taking adults. While some children and adults were returned after a while, there are many tales where they disappeared for good and never returned.

There are many mysterious tales of farmers being taken by wights to show the farmers how the cattle's droppings fell on their beds and food because the barn was built over the underground house of wights. In many cases, the farmers have moved the barn to a different place, to make sure the wights are not disturbed.

Another interesting story about wights is related to how they need a woman to do the job of a midwife in their world. The popular story among the Nordic people goes something like this: a woman was working in a barn when a strange man came running to her and worriedly asked her to help his wife. The strange man took the barn-worker through a door she had never seen before. They stepped into a beautiful home where a woman was in labor. The woman from the barn helped the pregnant lady give birth to her baby, wrapping up the child to keep it warm. After she stepped back out of the door, the barn-woman turned to see the door had disappeared completely, like it never existed. The next morning, the midwife found a big pile of silver spoons on her table. It was a gift of gratitude from the wights.

Stories abound of wights attending parties in the homes of human beings. They would come in hundreds, bring large amounts of food and drink with them, and leave without a trace when the party was over. However, there are also stories of wights being quite troublesome and not leaving when the party finished. Getting rid of these guests proved to be tricky. Stories of how such pesky wights would leave only when the names of Christian gods were uttered are plentiful in parts of Scandinavia.

Love stories between wights and humans also abound among the Asatru and Norse Pagan community. Sometimes, these love stories end happily with the human or the wight embracing and adopting his or her new home and identity. In some cases, the love stories end in tragedy and abandonment when one of the partners realizes that they are not of the same race as his or her love.

"The Wisdom of Odin" is a YouTube channel run by a follower of Norse Paganism named Jacob. He talks about his experiences with landvaettir and how he has befriended some of them. According to some believers of Norse Paganism, land spirits are there where gods cannot be. So, in some places where you cannot access pagan gods, you can access the land spirits and seek help if you need it.

Land spirits are tied to the land or place they live in, whereas the gods' control is vast. Land spirits are, therefore, handy and help to solve local problems. Land spirits open up channels through which we can connect with nature. Believers tend to make offerings to landvaettir in the form of fruit and vegetables. This ritual is symbolic of showing gratitude to nature for allowing us to access her abundance.

Because of this, such stories about wights thrive in Scandinavian folklore. Today, these stories are taken quite seriously and used as lessons not to harm or destroy nature. The philosophical connection between these folk tales and the power of nature is easy to see. The anger of the river when we abuse her power can be seen when she is flooding. Her destructive abilities can cause a lot of damage to human property and life, and it is her way of getting back at ruthless human beings who are insensitive to the importance of treating nature with respect and dignity.

Also, landslides and other natural disasters in places where humans excessively use natural resources are apparently further proof that wights who protect these elements of nature are angry with human beings and want to take revenge. When you treat nature with respect, she rewards you with abundance by allowing you to use her timber, agricultural produce, and other elements to prosper and be happy in your life.

Stories of wights are not just mythical tales, they also carry vital lessons in humility and dignity for us human beings. Asatru's Nine Noble Virtues embody many of these life lessons taught to us by wights.

Vaettir are seen as friendly beings that are placed by the gods to look after the regions they live in and protect the areas used by human beings. These beings guard and bless the endeavors of human beings, including farming, fishing, hunting, etc., as long as we do not give in to greed and willfully misuse the power of nature.

Other Nature Spirits

Elves – Elves were very important nature spirits for the Germanic people in the pre-Christian era. The popular version that elves are tricky and demonic beings is not really true. They are associated with goddess Freya and the seidr magic that she practices.

Alfar – In Heathenry, this term refers to the male ancestral lineage, but this Old Norse word literally translates to "elf." The Alfar finds mention in Sigvatr Thordarson's poem, "Austrfaravisur," in which he describes the Alfablot, a sacrificial ritual prevalent in ancient Sweden wherein strangers who visit farmsteads are sacrificed to the gods.

Also, Snorri Sturluson speaks of many kinds of elves, such as Dokkalfar, Svartalfar, and Ljossalfar in his work *Prose Edda*. Today, most Heathens believe that Alfar could be the spirits of our dead ancient ancestors who have been buried under the Earth for so long that they have become spirits.

Dwarfs – Dwarfs are frequently spoken of as being synonymous with Dokkalfar and Svartalfar. They are considered to be highly skilled in craftsmanship. They are credited with crafting many important items that are owned and used extensively by the gods and goddesses. In the *Prose Edda*, four dwarfs represent the four cardinal directions and are responsible for holding up the sky in place.

Interestingly, none of the authentic Norse mythological tales describe dwarfs as being ugly and squatty, the most popular depiction of dwarfs. They are described the same as elves are described in these Old Norse stories.

In summary, land spirits live in particular places and/or in some land features like rivers, hills, and mountains. They influence the wellbeing of the land that they rule over and have the power to curse or bless the people who live in that particular place or depend on that piece of land for anything. They are fierce protectors of the land they dwell in and are quite intolerant toward people who abuse or disrespect nature.

Chapter 7: Yggdrasil and the Nine Worlds

The cosmology of Asatru revolves around the World Tree referred to as Yggdrasil. The different realms are created around this magnificent tree. This chapter is dedicated to the Yggdrasil and the Nine Worlds of Asatru Cosmology.

The ancient Nordic people did not see the cosmos as only the Earth surrounded by the heavens above and the underworld or hell below. According to Asatru, the cosmos was a complex system of multiple realms and planes, including the human realm. All these planes of creation were interconnected with each other.

Before the start of time, Muspelheim, the fiery realm of fire, which was in the south, moved north to meet Niflheim, the icy realm. They met at Ginnungagap or the yawning void, and their powers combined. Muspelheim and Niflheim's union brought forth two beings, Ymir (whom we have spoken about in an earlier chapter) and Audhumla, a primeval cow of gigantic proportions.

The primeval cow licked the ice and created a new being named Buri, and from Buri came Borr. Marriages among these early beings, as well as sexless reproduction by Ymir, resulted in multiple generations of beings until three godly beings, namely Odin, Villi, and Ve, killed Ymir and created the cosmos from his body parts. The cosmos created from Ymir's body parts consisted of the World Tree and the Nine Worlds. The World Tree, Yggdrasil, supported the Nine Worlds, who were separated by vast distances.

Rivers, valleys, hills, and mountains separated the Nine Worlds and were formed between them by the bark of the World Tree. According to Norse Paganism, the entire cosmos is much bigger than the Nine Worlds centered on the Yggdrasil. There are unknown worlds beyond the enclosure of the Nine Worlds. The Nine Worlds of the cosmos of Norse Paganism were:

- *Asgard* - The realm of the Aesir gods and goddesses.

- *Muspelheim* - The realm of the primal fire and the place where the Muspilli fire giants live.

- *Niflheim* - The realm of the primal snow or ice and the world of mists.

- *Jotunheim* - The realm of the giants and the jotnar.

- *Alfheim* - The realm of the Light Elves.

- *Hel or Helheim* - The realm of the dead.

- *Vanaheim* - The realm of the Vanir gods and goddesses.

- *Svartalfheim* - The realm of the dwarfs and black elves.

- *Midgard* - The realm of human beings.

Each of these nine realms has specific kinds of spiritual-psychological elements in operation. Let us look at the Yggdrasil and the Nine Worlds in a bit of detail.

The Yggdrasil

The Yggdrasil is the World Tree or the Tree of Life. This gigantic tree rises from the Well of Wyrd and forms the framework of the Nine-World cosmos accessible to the beings of Norse Pagans. The Nine Worlds reside in Yggdrasil's branches and roots. The World Tree serves as a conduit for travelers to move from one world to another.

Yggdrasil is frequently described as an ash tree, although it bears fruit and needles too. Most believers accept that Yggdrasil is a tree that cannot be compared with anything seen or known in the human world. Alternately, Yggdrasil could be a tree that combines the power and capabilities of all the mortal trees known to human beings.

Yggdrasil literally translates to "Steed of Yggr" or "Odin's Horse." "Yggr" is one of the many names of Odin and means "the terrible one." This name referred to the episode in Odin's life when he spent nine days and nine nights hanging on the World Tree to gain knowledge and wisdom until the Runes were finally revealed to him. Interestingly, an ancient Germanic custom of hanging sacrificial victims from trees could be rooted in Odin's self-sacrifice episode. Archeological evidence of the "Tollund Man" found in 1950 in a Jutland peat bog points to this kind of old Germanic custom.

The discovered body was so excellently preserved that it was possible to deduce that he was hanged ritually and then buried in the bog. This was the second such body to be discovered. About a hundred yards away, another body of a ritually hanged woman was also excavated.

A poem in the *Poetic Edda* called "Fjolsvinnsmal" refers to the Tree of Life as Mimir's Tree or Mimameid. It is also known as Lerad, a tree so huge that its twigs and leaves provide food for the goat, Heidrun, and the stag, Eikþyrnir, that live on the roof of Valhalla.

Three roots support the Yggdrasil. One of these roots passes through Asgard. The second one passes through Jotunheim, and the third one goes through Helheim. The sacred Well of Wyrd where the three Norns or Nornir (the three Fates) lived was beneath Asgard's roots. Even the gods had no control over the Well of Wyrd. The Well of Mimir (or Memory), Mimisbrunnr, lay beneath the root of Jotunheim while the well Hvergelmir (or the Roaring Cauldron) lay beneath the Helheim root.

The World Tree is an essential element to the story of Ragnarok. According to prophecies in Norse mythology, only two human beings would survive the Ragnarok, namely Lif and Lifthrasir. These two people would escape from the brunt of the war by sheltering themselves in Yggdrasil's branches and consuming the dew on the World Tree leaves.

Muspelheim

Muspelheim is the realm of fire and home to the fire giants; ruled over by Surtr or the Black one. It is located to the south of Ginnungagap. In Norse mythology, fire giants like Surtr are considered to be as close to pure evil as possible. Muspelheim, along with Niflheim (the realm of ice), joined together to create the first being: Ymir. It is believed that sparks from this realm created comets, stars, and planets. According to some sources of Norse mythology, Muspelheim fire giants are expected to fight against the gods in Ragnarok.

Niflheim

Niflheim or "Mistland" is the realm of cold and ice. Located to the north of Ginnungagap, Niflheim is inhabited by ice giants or Rimtursir. Niflheim is ruled over by Hel, daughter of Loki and a giantess. Odin appoints Hel to rule over Niflheim. Half of Hel's body is normal, while the other half resembles a rotting corpse.

Niflheim is divided into numerous sub-realms, out of which one of the realms is dedicated to gods and heroes. In this sub-realm, the goddess Hel presides over the festivities held for the gods and heroes. Another sub-layer of Niflheim is for the sick, elderly, and all those who cannot die in glory. The ones who die in glory go straight to Valhalla in Asgard.

The lowest sub-realm in Niflheim is similar to the hell in Christianity reserved for the wicked who will rot here for eternity. Niflheim is located beneath the third root of Yggdrasil and close to the river Hvergelmir or the "stream that bubbles and boils" and the sunless hall or Nastrand, which means "corpse strands."

In terms of philosophy and psychology, Niflheim is the plane of evolutionary impulse or telekinesis.

Asgard

The Aesir gods and goddesses' realm is Asgard, and it is fortified by strong walls built by a frost giant and guarded by Heimdall. The plain of Idavoll lies right at the center of Asgard, and this is the place where the deities meet for important discussions. Two important halls in Asgard are Vingolf, where the goddesses meet, and Gladsheim, where the gods meet. Valhalla, or the hall of the slain, is another hall of importance in Asgard. The warriors killed in battle are guided to Valhalla by the Valkyries, where they are prepared for the Ragnarok.

Asgard is at a higher plane than Midgard. Human beings can reach Asgard in multiple ways, including:

- The Bifrost or Asbru, a rainbow bridge that connects Midgard to Asgard.

- Gjallerbru or the resounding bridge in Helheim.

- Myrkvid or the mirk wood between Muspelheim and Asgard.

- The rivers flowing around Asgard. Thor uses these rivers, as the bridges cannot withstand his weight.

Asgard is believed to symbolize the highest levels of consciousness.

Vanaheim

Home to the Vanir gods and goddesses, Vanaheim is also close to Asgard and is one of the highest planes in the cosmology of Norse Paganism. Vanaheim is also referred to as the home of the Earth deities of fertility. The Vanir gods are believed to be more benevolent and compassionate than the Aesir gods, who are more passionate and love wars and battles.

The three prominent deities of Vanaheim are Njord, Freyr, and Freya. Vanaheim is full of beautiful mansions and palaces, similar to Asgard. Vanaheim is the birthplace of Njord, and he would return here after Ragnarok, one of the few gods and goddesses who was prophesized to survive the end of the world.

Jotunheim

Jotunheim is the realm of the giants and the jotnar. The giants create menacing problems for the people in Midgard and the gods in Asgard. A river called Irving separates Asgard and Jotunheim. The most important city in the realm of the giants is Utgard.

Utgard is the primary stronghold of the giants from where Loki ruled over the realm. Loki was a devious, dangerous, and powerful giant who appears in numerous stories as Thor's friend and companion. Utgard means "the world outside the enclosure" and is home to evil beings. Asgard and Midgard are seen as places shared by and accessible to both gods and humans, whereas Utgard is seen as the divider and is viewed as an ocean or river.

Other important places in Jotunheim are Thrymheim (the dwelling of Thiai) and Gastropnir (the dwelling of Menglad). It also houses the Jarnvid or the "ironwood." According to mythology, Jotunheim is in the north of Midgard. From a philosophical perspective, Jotunheim is the realm of might and force.

Alfheim

Alfheim is the home of the bright or light elves and is believed to be a place of splendid beauty. The elves residing in Alfheim are also considered to be very beautiful. Very close to Asgard, Alfheim is full of meadows, forests, and beautiful islands amidst large seas. It is considered to be a happy, sunny place.

The Elven race residing in Alfheim is similar to human beings, although they are taller, fairer, and live longer than humans. Alfheim was a gift given to Freyr when he was an infant and got his first tooth. Alfheim is the domain of the ego and the place of intuition and instinctive powers.

Midgard

Midgard is the realm of human beings and is believed to be located in the middle of the World Tree. Midgard translates to "the realm in the middle," which is the reason it is often referred to as the "Middle Earth."

Midgard is described as a middle world that exists between Helheim (hell or the underworld) and Asgard (the heavens or the upper world). Thus, Midgard forms part of a triad which includes:

- The upper realm, or the heavens.
- The middle realm, or the Earth.
- The lower realm, or the underworld.

Midgard was created from the flesh and blood of Ymir, the primal living being. Bifrost, the rainbow bridge guarded by Heimdall, connects Midgard to Asgard. A gigantic ocean where Jormungand the great snake resides surrounds Midgard. It is so huge and long that it encircles Midgard entirely and ends up biting its own tail.

Thor is the son of the Earth Goddess, and therefore, he took it upon himself to protect the people of Midgard. Being an Aesir god, he also became the self-appointed protector of Asgard. Thor was, therefore, the powerful protector of Midgard and Asgard against the marauding beings who sought to harm the two worlds closest to Thor's heart.

According to Norse mythology, Midgard was completely decimated in Ragnarok. Jormungand emerged from the vast seas surrounding Midgard to poison the land and waters with its venom. The sea lashed up against the land. In the final battle, almost all life on Midgard was destroyed, and the sea swallowed up the earth.

Midgard is associated with our conscious thought, the area of the mind that human being's access when we are awake. This realm also represents the path of spiritual and genetic evolution, individual growth, and the synergy of light and darkness as well as fire and ice.

Helheim

Helheim or Hel is the realm or abode of the dead. The Goddess Hel or Hella rules over it, and it's the lowest realm of the Nine Worlds. Resting far beneath the Yggdrasil, it is close to Niflheim. Not all parts of Helheim are bad and dark. Some parts are like an afterlife paradise filled with light and happiness and some parts of it are dark and gloomy.

Also, Hel is not a place of punishment. Primarily, it is a place where the souls of the dead rest. It is filled with the ghostly specters of souls that have died ingloriously or lived a wicked life. Helheim is also the home of souls who have broken promises in their lives.

Helheim is reached through three portals, including:

- The Hell Way or Highway to Hell or Helvergr.
- Gjoll, a river of blood.
- Gnipahellier or Overhanging cave.

The gateway to Hel is called Hel's Gate (Helgrind) or Corpse Gate (Nagrind), which is guarded by Modgud, a giantess along with her giant hound, Garmr. The gates of hell are toward the south, away from Asgard, whose gates are to the north. Gjoll, the river of blood surrounding Hel, is freezing cold and also has knives floating on it.

The only way one can cross the river is by walking across a bridge that is guarded by a giantess. According to Norse Paganism beliefs, if a living person walked on the bridge, it would create noise so loud that it seemed as if a thousand men were trying to walk on it, but a dead person could walk across the bridge without a sound.

In the northern part of Hel the mansion of the goddess Hel is located, which is called Evdinir or "misery." A wall called the "falling peril" or Fallanda Forad surrounds goddess Hel's palace. Below Hel's mansion is the place of punishment for the wicked called Kvalheim, and located here is a place made of adders or snakes. The wicked and evil people are sent here so that the poison of the snake drips on them.

Psychologically and philosophically speaking, Helheim refers to the collective unconscious aspects of the human mind. It also represents the human connection with nature and our ancestors.

Svartalfheim

Svartalfheim is the realm of the black elves (the light elves live in Alfheim). Black or dark elves are known as Dokkalfar in Norse mythology. Like the trolls, the dark elves are connected with "daveves" or "dvergar." Some sources state that this realm can be accessed through certain caves in Midgard.

As defined by Norse Paganism, the cosmos is based around Yggdrasil and comprises the Nine Worlds that spread across the branches and roots of this magical tree.

Chapter 8: Heathen Rituals, Shamans, and Songs

This chapter is dedicated to heathen rites and rituals and how they have undergone changes in modern times, even as new lessons, especially compassionate ideas, were learned and incorporated into the ancient culture. We start the chapter with the most important Asatru ritual—the blot.

The Blot

The blot is a Heathenry ritual where offerings are given to the gods. Exchanging gifts was an important aspect of early Germanic tribes and societies. Giving gifts was a way of making and maintaining friendships and relationships. Gift exchanges among family and kinsfolk were a way of bonding with each other and reflecting the responsibility of each member toward the community as a whole. Interestingly, the offering of gifts to gods and goddesses had the same connotation.

Norse Pagans believe that we are friends and kinsfolk of gods and goddesses. Heathens do not look upon their deities as masters, nor do they look upon themselves as being slaves to the gods. This approach means that the offering of gifts is not taken as a way of appeasing or pleasing the deities, but as a way of demonstrating kinship and friendship.

So, the next question is, what kind of gifts do the gods give to us? The Astruars believe that the most useful and important gifts we can get from our gods are courage, wisdom, spiritual insights and growth, a feeling of connection with nature and the cosmos, inspiration, and awe and gratitude for what we have access to in this world. Good luck is also an important gift that gods can give human beings.

Human beings give gifts of loyalty ("troth" is the archaic term used by Heathens), honor, and remembrance. The mutual exchange of gifts creates a rich and deep bond between gods and human beings and is beneficial to everyone concerned.

In addition to being a gift-giving ritual for the gods, a blot ceremony provides an opportunity for believers to get together and bond over their culture and tradition. The ritual typically happens outdoors and includes an offering of mead, which is kept in a bowl. For the uninitiated, mead is an alcoholic beverage made by fermenting honey with water and often flavored with fruits, hops, grains, and spices.

In a blot ceremony, the priests and/or priestesses invoke the gods and seek their help. They then use a branch or sprig of an evergreen tree to sprinkle mead on the idols of the deities. The offering is also sprinkled on the assembled participants. The ritual could be improvised as it progresses, or the priests and priestesses could follow a strict structure and script. There are no hard and fast rules for it.

When the sprinkling is done, and the gods invoked, the bowl of mead is emptied into the fire or the earth, signifying the final libation. Often, the blot ritual is followed by a communal meal, which forms part of the ritual itself.

Other simpler forms of blot rituals are also followed. For example, the concerned practitioner might simply keep aside some food for the gods and wights without the use of sacred words or incantations. Some practicing Asatruars and Heathens perform simple daily rituals in their homes, but for most people, blot ceremonies are performed only on special occasions.

Changes in the Ritual Over Time – In ancient times (during the Iron Age) as well as during the Middle Ages, the term "blot" referred to rituals involving animal sacrifices as a way of sending gratitude to the gods in return for favors received, but such kinds of sacrificial rites and rituals are inconvenient for modern practitioners and not aligned to their morals and principles.

Moreover, animal slaughter in most countries is highly regulated by the government under humaneness and compassionate guidelines, along with hygiene considerations. In fact, the Astruars of Iceland explicitly reject animal sacrifices of all kinds. There are many instances of sacrifices gone wrong, wherein the animals were not slain correctly and died in agony.

Therefore, nearly all modern practitioners accept the belief that such instances are signs of displeasure from the gods, which, in turn, could drive them to cause harm to the practitioners and their families as a way of punishment. And so, animal sacrifices are not part of the modern blot ritual.

The modern-day blot ritual is quite easy and uncomplicated and can be practiced by everyone. It is a two-part process, particularly:

- We give our gifts to the gods.
- The gods give their gifts to us.

In the first part, the worshippers fill the drinking horn with mead. This horn is passed around the circle of worshippers who have gathered for the ritual. Each member holds the horn with both hands. This stance reflects the transfer of the gifts of love, honor, and loyalty from the holder's spirit through the hands, then to the horn, and from there to the gods. As the drinking horn moves around the circle, each worshipper transfers his or her love, devotion, and loyalty to the drinking horn.

When the circle is complete, the drinking horn is given to the person who is officiating the blot ritual. He or she raises the horn (filled with the love and loyalty of the worshippers) and offers the gifts up to the gods and goddesses. The remaining mead is then poured out as a final libation to the gods. An important point to note is that the mead itself is not the gift. It is only a medium that holds the gifts of love, devotion, and loyalty of the worshippers to their gods.

The second part of the blot ritual involves receiving the gifts and blessings from the gods and goddesses in return. Again, the drinking horn is filled with mead. The officiating priest or priestess raises the horn high again so that the gods can infuse the mead with their powers and blessings, might, inspiration, spiritual guidance, and other gifts.

Now, these gifts and blessings from the gods and goddesses need to be shared among the worshippers. There are two ways that an officiating person can perform this ritual. In one method, the priest or priestess takes a big bowl, pours the blessed and empowered mead into it, takes a sprig or branch of an evergreen tree, dips it into the mead, and sprinkles it on all the participants and worshippers. The sprinkling symbolizes the transfer of the power of the gods to the people present in the ritual.

Another method is to pass the drinking horn filled with the consecrated mead from member to member so that he or she can drink the empowered liquid and get a share of the power of the gods and goddesses.

Blots can be offered to multiple gods and goddesses simultaneously, or to a specific god or deity for a specific wish or need to be fulfilled. While modern-day gifts from gods and goddesses are intangible elements like courage, honor, good luck, etc., in the olden days, blots were performed for victory in battle, a safe voyage, a good harvest, prosperity, and other tangible needs and desires of the worshippers.

In a modern context, our battles do not need axes and bows and arrows. But we still have our own daily battles to fight. It is perfectly natural to seek help from the divine beings to win such battles, and blots are a great way to commune with the gods and ask for their help in the form of wisdom and good luck.

A Simple Guide to a Blot Ritual

This section contains a detailed explanation of how to conduct a blot ritual in your own way to reconnect with your ancestors, gods, and deities and reach out to them for their help. A perfect setting for a blot ritual is amidst the beauty and splendor of nature. Here is a step-by-step guide to help you get started.

First, you must prepare for the ritual. Then, the actual ritual has nine components, including:

1. *Vigia* – The dedication.

2. *Helgia* – The consecration.

3. *Bidja* – The prayer.

4. *Blota (Also Called Offra)* – The offering.

5. *Senda* – The sending.

6. *Signa* – The blessing.

7. *Kjosa* – The choosing.

8. *Soa* – The consuming.

9. *Enda* – The closing.

Before we can go into these nine parts, it is essential that you get the setting or the location right for the ritual. The best and most ideal place for a blot would be a grove or amidst nature. It is vital that you feel a sacred and solemn connection to the location where you want to conduct the blot ritual. A few examples of such ideal locations are:

- A large tree that reflects the power and strength of nature.

- Near a running body of water that mimics the fountains of the heavens and the underworld.

- The top of a mountain, which signifies the site of Valhalla.

Certain trees have great significance in Norse Paganism. The oak tree is connected to Thor, the ash tree reflects the World Tree, and the yew tree is related to death and transformation. Another important element for a blot ritual is privacy. You must choose a place where strangers cannot walk in unannounced and suddenly interrupt the ritual.

Now, it is not always possible to find a place outdoors that suits all these requirements, especially in modern times; a temple or hof would be a great location. If there is no Asatru hof in your area or community, you can create a sacred place in your own home, centered around a "stalli," or a sacred altar, for the blot ritual.

Once you have settled on the location, then it is time to move on to the next step which is to gather the tools needed for the ritual, which include the following:

- Statues or idols of gods and goddesses you will be dedicating the ritual to and praying to. These idols are an excellent way to get your focus on the rite, and it gives you a sense of having your deities present with you during the ceremony. While it is not possible or practical to have the idols of the entire range of the pantheon of gods and goddesses, you can choose to have a couple that you feel connected with and use the same idols for the rituals.

- Mead is an important element of any blot right from ancient times. It was believed that honey mead was very sacred to the gods, as it had its origins in the fountains of the underworld. While there are commercially available meads, it would be special if you brewed your own at home.

- The three important tools for the mead include the drinking horn, blot bowl, and the "hlauteinn." The drinking horn made of cattle horn dates back to ancient Roman times. The blot bowl is needed to pour the mead later during the ritual. The "hlauteinn" is an evergreen sprig used to sprinkle the consecrated mead on the worshippers. Before you cut a sprig from the tree, it is vital that you ask permission from the tree by offering a libation of mead to the chosen tree.

Other tools used during the rite include:

- A sacrificial blade to cut the offering (in the days of animal sacrifice). This blade was used to scrape out the runes, too, as the incantations and prayers were recited.

- A ritual hammer invoking the power and might of Thor's Mjolnir, which was used to hallow items and elements throughout the ritual.

- A gandr, which is a staff or wand, which was charged and used for special purposes.

- The need-fire (a filament flame) contained in a portable lantern.

- The peord or a special box to hold rune tablets.

The runes can be inscribed using the sacrificial blade onto any sacred object or a piece of wood. For example, in ancient times, warriors would carve the runes on their weapons for victory in battle. Sailors would carve them on oars for a safe voyage. Midwives would tattoo or paint the runes on their hands, seeking help from the gods to guide them through deliveries safely.

The runes you choose should be directly related to your prayers and needs. It could be one or two rune letters related to the ritual, or it could be the spelling of a word in prayer. A commonly carved rune is the word "alu," which translates to spiritual ecstasy. Even each rune alphabet has its own significance. For example, the rune "Ass" or "Ansuz" relates to the gods' spiritual wisdom. If you are going to carve the runes on a piece of wood, then it would be good to choose the wood from the tree whose significance is connected to your prayer.

Once you have carved the runes on the object or piece of wood, use the sacrificial blade and scrape the runes into the mead, signifying the transfer of power from the runes into the mead. The next step of preparation is the use of the ritual hammer signifying Thor's Mjolnir, the most important tool of consecration in Norse Paganism. The hammersign ritual finds mention in the early texts dating back to ancient times.

If you don't have a ceremonial hammer, you can use your fist for this step. The hammersign ritual starts with placing the hammer or your fist on your forehead, saying loudly and boldly, "ODIN!" As you perform the hammersign at each place, feel the power of the Aesir gods flowing through your body and mind.

Now, move the hammer to your solar plexus area and say, "BALDER!" Then, take it to your left shoulder and say, "FREY." Move it to the right shoulder and say, "THOR." Finally, touch the object that needs to be consecrated and say, "Vingthorshammar Vigia" which translates to "The Hallowing Hammer of Thor, Consecrate!" This ritual makes our object holy and it is believed to be under Thor's protection and that of his powerful hammer.

The next step is to set up the altar or "stalli." The altar is the central focus of the blot and signifies Asgard, the home of the gods. A white linen cloth to cover your altar gives it a clean, aesthetically pleasing look. Lighting a couple of candles enhances the sacredness of the "stalli." You can arrange all the tools and elements on the altar in an orderly manner, assuring there is no clutter.

When your preparations are done, you can begin the 9-step blot ritual process as follows:

Vigia - The Dedication: A blot begins with a dedication of the altar and the ritual's sacred space to the gods or vigia. The officiating priest or priestess sends up prayers of dedication to the gods in the form of songs or hallowed verses, while the other participants use various responses at the end of each hallowed verse. Here is a simple example of a hallowed verse you can use in the dedication step:

> "We call upon all the deities and ancestors,
>
> To come and dwell in this hallowed space.
>
> To be with us while we honor you with our gifts,
>
> And give us the help and gifts we seek."

Helgia - The Consecration: In the consecration process, the sacred fire purifies the air of the sacred space where the ritual is taking place. The need-fire is carried around the perimeter of the ritual space as a hallowed verse is chanted by the participants and/or the officiating priest or priestess.

The need-fire is taken three times around the perimeter of the sacred space, and for each revolution, the hallowed verse is chanted three times. Hence, the hallowed verse is chanted nine times. Nine is the most sacred number in Asatru. An example of the consecration verse can be something like this:

> "We call upon the loving and noble gods and goddesses,
>
> To light up and sanctify this area of prayer,
>
> Keep it sacred and holy,
>
> And give us your blessings to complete what we have started."

Bidja – The Prayer: The bidja is the holy prayer of the blot ritual. It is usually performed with the rune Elgr or Elhaz. The participants stand erect and raise their arms over their heads in a "Y" formation as they focus on the idols of the deities on the altar. This segment is about connecting with the deities and gods of the ritual within the perimeter of the sanctified area. An example of a hallowed verse in prayer can be created based on your need at the time. Here is an example of a prayer of protection chanted during the blot ritual during Winter Nights:

"O powerful and mighty Thor,

Grant us protection and peace.

Winter is upon us, give us courage and strength.

Keep us safe and warm."

You can have hallowed verses to each god whose help is being sought in the ritual.

Blota (Also Called Offra) – The Offering: This step concerns the offering to the gods, which is the central part of the blot ritual. Different offerings are given to different gods depending on the needs and time of the year. While animal sacrifices were part of the ritual in ancient times, in modern days, mead is the most common and popular offering. Odin is believed to live and survive on honey mead only, and therefore, it is considered an ideal offering to the gods in any ritual.

Before offering the mead to the gods, you need to charge it with the hammersign. This consecrated mead is offered up in an offering bowl or the drinking horn with a hallowed verse, an example of which is below:

"Gods and Goddesses of Asgard,

Your friends from Midgard offer these gifts to you,

In return for your protection and love,

Accept this offering of gratitude and reverent devotion."

Senda - The Sending: Now, it is time to send the offerings to the gods. There are many ways to do so, and all of them use the four elements, including fire, water, earth, and air, to send the offerings. In ancient times (thanks to archeological evidence), we know that plates of offerings were submerged in water, buried under the earth, left hanging from a tree, or put into the sacrificial fire. Today, it is a common practice to pour the offering of mead on the earth so that it finds its way to the gods. An example of a hallowed verse for this procedure could be as follows:

> "We send these offerings to you,
>
> That will find their way to your homes in the heavens,
>
> Partake of our gifts,
>
> And watch and protect our world."

Signa - The Blessing: According to Norse gift exchange traditions, it is now time to receive our gifts from the gods in return for our gifts to them. The officiating priest or priestess dips the evergreen sprig into the mead in the offering bowl and sprinkles it on all of the assembled people. An example of a hallowed verse for this occasion is given below:

> "Hail to you, almighty gods and goddesses,
>
> We solemnly thank you for your blessings.
>
> All through the branches of Yggdrasil,
>
> May you always hear our call."

Kjosa - The Choosing: This step is about interpreting the message of the gods. In a blot ritual, the lot box or peord filled with runes is first offered to the gods seeking their message.

> "We offer these runes to you, mighty gods,
>
> We seek your message for us, powerful gods,
>
> Tell us what we need to know,
>
> And bless us with your wisdom."

Then, each of the participants picks up one rune from the lot box. The interpretations of the rune they pick are then used as guidance points in their coming days.

Soa - The Consuming: Sumbel is a drinking ritual that is often performed to consume the consecrated mead. The sumbel is described in detail in the next section of this chapter.

Enda - The Closing: This entire blot ritual is now in the concluding stage. The officiating person performs a closing ceremony allowing everyone to return to their mundane, routine world after their communion with the world of gods and goddesses, leaving the participants empowered and strengthened. This step involves hailing and thanking the gods for spending time with the participants and seeking their permission to close the blot ceremony.

> "Hail to the gods who heard us,
>
> Hail to the goddesses who heard us,
>
> We thank you from the bottom of our hearts,
>
> Watch over us and our world."

Sumbel

Sumbel is another common drinking ritual followed by practicing Heathens. Also spelled as symbel, this is a ritual drinking ceremony in which the practitioners raise a toast to their gods. Often, a sumbel follows a blot ritual and involves a drinking horn in which the consecrated and blessed mead is filled. The drinking horn is passed among the assembled practitioners three times, signifying the past, present, and future.

Odinshorn signifies our past, Thorshorn our present, and Freyshorn, our future. Some of the practitioners sip directly from the drinking horn or pour a little of the drink into their own glasses, and as each person does so, he or she makes a comment or a toast to the gods, according to his or her needs.

During the sumbel ceremony, toasts are made to the gods, goddesses, and deities. Verbal tributes are also made to the ancestors, gods, and heroes from Norse mythology. After this, oaths are taken with regard to future actions. Oaths and promises made during such ceremonies are considered binding for the oath-takers, thanks to the high level of sacredness rendered to the sumbel ceremony.

In a sumbel ceremony, the toasts made to the gods and the tributes paid to the ancestors help the worshippers connect with and harness their powers and use them in their own lives. In modern times, sumbel has a powerful social role to play in Heathenry. It is a place and time when bonds are cemented, political moves are made, peace is negotiated, and newfound relationships and partnerships are forged in the Heathen community.

Sumbel ceremonies are conducted with a focus on children, too, for which the drinking horn is filled with apple juice instead of mead. During the toast paying tributes to the gods, children tape pictures of apples onto a poster of a tree, which symbolizes the apple tree of Goddess Idunn.

At this point, it might make sense to summarize the differences between sumbel and blot in Asatru. A blot is a ceremonial prayer that can range from a simple individual ritual wherein only the practitioner lifts a mug of coffee or drink to share with the gods, to a large community event that happens on a football field. The small blot can be done individually at home regularly, while formalized Heathenism organizations handle the bigger ones.

Sumbel, on the other hand, is like a sacred drinking party where gods are toasted, and the participants sing their tributes even as the drinking horn is passed around. Each person takes oaths and boasts as the drinking horn is passed around. A group blot is an awe-inspiring experience, while a sumbel is a great bonding experience for practitioners.

Seidr and Galdr

Seidr is a religious practice in Heathenism that consists of a shamanic ritual trance. Scholars tend to believe that modern seidr practices could have been developed during the 1990s when Neo-Shamanism was developed and popularized, though older forms of seidr are described in many sagas. One of the most popular seidr practices of the ancient followers of Norse Paganism is referred to as oracular or high-seat seidr, which is described in Eiriks saga or the Saga of Erik the Red. This saga is an account of the exploration of North America by the Nordic people.

In the oracular seidr ritual, a seidr practitioner sits on a high seat. Chants and songs are used to invoke the gods and wights. Drumming, a popular element in Shamanism, is used to induce an altered state of consciousness in the practitioner. In this altered state of consciousness, the practitioner undertakes a meditative journey where they travel through the World Tree to Helheim.

The assembled participants ask questions to which they need answers. The practitioner finds these answers from Helheim by speaking to the ancestor spirits, and the divine beings that reside there pass the messages and answers on to the seekers. Some seidr practitioners use entheogenic substances to achieve an altered state of consciousness.

Glade is another Asatru practice that involves singing and chanting rune names and rune poems. Runic alphabets were used to write Germanic languages before the Christian influence. Chanting and reciting these poems rhythmically in a community helps participants get into altered states of consciousness, which, in turn, helps them to seek out deities and communicate with them. Although these poems were written in a Christian context, most practitioners believe that the themes reflected in them are of a pre-Christian era. Moreover, some poems are re-appropriated for modern Heathenism.

Festivals of Heathenism

In addition to the various blot rituals, different groups of Heathens celebrate different festivals based on their belief systems and cultures. The most common Heathen festivals celebrated by most groups include:

Winter Nights – Also known as vetrnaetr in the Old Norse language, Winter Nights refers to a three-day festival that marks the start of winter. Specific sacrifices and rituals are held during Winter Nights.

In the olden days, the King of Sweden performed a public sacrifice as part of a community event called disablot. Contrarily, alfablot was a ritual and/or sacrifice of the ancient times carried out in each household privately for specific local spirits and family deities.

Yule – Yule or Yuletide is connected to Odin, but the Christianization of this festival has resulted in Christmastide. Many customs and traditions practiced during Christmas today, including Yule goat, Yule log, and Yule singing, are borrowed from Norse Pagan cultures, or so it is believed. The above festivals find mention in Heimskringla and therefore, are believed to be of ancient origins.

Rituals and rites were an integral part of ancient Norse Paganism and adorn the modern version of Asatru. Sacred and hallowed verses, beautifully crafted ritual tools, food and drink, a deep sense of bonding and connection with other believers and the gods and goddesses, etc., drive present-day Asatruars to keep the tradition of rituals and ceremonies alive.

Chapter 9: Celebrate Like a Heathen – Holidays and Festivals

Celebrations and festivals are an integral part of Heathenism, and the Heathen calendar is replete with feast days, memorial days, and other special occasions. In fact, keeping and performing festivals is one of the primary duties of an Asatruar. Keeping these important days reflects the respect and love for their ancestors, gods, and goddesses.

Celebrating festivals and commemorating our ancestors and gods fills us with a deep sense of sacredness and takes us closer to the spirits of our ancestors and our deities. When we remember them on special days, they return the gift by providing us with protection, strength, and courage.

Most of our festival and feast days are aligned with the agricultural patterns of our culture and tradition, which, in turn, align our lives with the dynamism of climate and weather changes. Accordingly, every festival, feast, and ritual represents a transformation of the Earth as well as our souls.

Asatru has a compilation of all the feasts and festivals of all the Germanic and Nordic tribes that were considered important right throughout Northern Europe. In ancient times, some tribes kept certain feasts while others kept other festivals. The important thing about festivals in Asatru is not the time or even the ritual. It is more about the gods, goddesses, and ancestors who are hailed and worshipped as the Earth transforms around us. Let us look at some traditional festivals of Asatru in detail, although a couple of them were discussed briefly in the previous chapter.

Yule or Yuletide – The 12-Day Festival

The festival of Yule starts approximately on December 20th and goes on until the beginning of the next year. The word Yule is derived from "hjol," an Old Norse language term meaning "wheel." This is the period when the year's wheel is at its lowest point and is set to rise again.

"Hjol" or wheel is a direct reference to the Sun as a fiery wheel that rolls across the sky. It is important to note here that Yuletide celebrations predate Christmas and Christianity by thousands of years. Ancient Icelandic sagas are replete with references to Yuletide and also have descriptions of how this festival was celebrated. Yuletide was a time of joy, festivities, exchanging of gifts, dancing, and singing.

The holidays of Yuletide were considered to be the most sacred amongst all ancient Germanic tribes. According to Norse Paganism, this period marks the return of Balder from Helheim. It also marks the beginning of the end of freezing winters. The start of the Yuletide festival has no fixed date. But it is typically celebrated for twelve days and usually begins at sunset on the day of the Winter Solstice (the longest night and the shortest day of the year), which normally falls on December 20th in the Northern Hemisphere.

The first night of the Yuletide is called Mother's Night when Frigg and female ancestor spirits (collectively called Disir) are honored. The name also refers to the rebirth of the world from the darkness of winter. A nightlong traditional vigil is kept on Mother's Night to make certain that the Sun will rise again after the darkest night and to warmly welcome it.

The Norse deities are called Yule-Beings because, during this twelve-day period, they are closest to Midgard, the human realm. This is the season when even the dead return to Earth and participate in the festivities. Importantly, magical beings like trolls and elves roam freely, which can be dangerous for human beings. Therefore, the Asatruars believe in appeasing these beings with offerings of food and drink. The Yuletide period was a time of baking bread, cookies, cakes, and decorating every Heathen's home.

Disting

Disting (or Disablot) is a regular festival in Sweden (in this country, it was the first public fair or assembly of the year) and is also referred to as "Charming of the Plow." This ceremony takes place at the end of January or in the first or second week of February. In Denmark, the Disting festival is marked by the activity of furrowing the fields for the first time in the year. It is a feast signifying new beginnings. The ritual involves prayers to the gods seeking blessings before starting the work for the year.

Ostara – March 20th–21st

The Ostara signifies the Spring Equinox and is celebrated on March 21 every year. Marking the start of the summer months, it is named after the goddess Ostara, an important Germanic deity who embodied spring and the renewal and revival of life. The name Ostara signifies the east and glory.

The Ostara festival is a celebration of the revival of the Earth after months of freezing cold winters. Traditionally, homes are decorated with flowered, colored eggs, budding boughs, and branches, etc. The hare was the spirit animal or holy beast of the goddess Ostara. Slaying and eating rabbit meat was permitted only after taking permission from the goddess.

Holding and keeping the Ostara feast enhances the joy and happiness of the festival participants.

Some common folklore traditions that have carried on from ancient times and continue even today include:

- Fires kindled at the top of hills at the break of dawn.

- The performance of plays in villages and rural areas. In these plays, summer and winter are shown as people battling with each other, with summer winning over winter and driving him off of the stage.

- Effigies signifying winter as drowned, beaten, and burned to signify the end of winter.

Walpurgis Night or May Eve

Different countries celebrate it on different days, ranging from April 30th to May 1st. In Germany, Finland, and Sweden, May Eve is celebrated on April 30th. This festival is named after a lady called Valborg or Walpurgis or Valderburger or Wealdburg. She was born in 710 in Britain and was Saint Boniface's niece. She and her brother, Wunibald, traveled to Wurttemberg, Germany, where Wunibald founded the Convent of Heidenheim. His sister, Walpurgis, became a nun in this convent. She died in 779 and was anointed as a saint on May 1st of the same year.

Viking fertility festivals used to be celebrated on April 30th, and because Walpurgis was declared a saint at the same time, her name became connected with Viking fertility celebrations. Walpurgis was worshipped, similar to the way Vikings celebrated spring.

Walpurgis is one of the primary national holidays in Finland and Sweden, along with Midsummer and Yuletide. Large bonfires are lit, and the young people are tasked with collecting branches, wildflowers, and greens from the woods, which are then used to decorate the village homes. The young people are rewarded with eggs.

Heathens believe that Freya is the ruler of this festival because Walpurgis is the Germanic equivalent of Valentine's Day, and Freya is the goddess of love and witchcraft. In Scandinavia, the May Tree is taken out in a procession during this festival, a tradition that goes back to the fruitfulness procession of ancient Heathens. Fires are built in high places at night, and people jump over the flames for luck and good fortune.

Midsummer – Summer Solstice June 20th–21st

Midsummer is a Heathen religious celebration held at the Summer Solstice (the longest day and the shortest night of the year), which falls on either June 20th or 21st. Midsummer's Eve is believed to be the second most important Germanic festival after the Yuletide. On this day, the Northern Hemisphere is most tilted toward the sun.

Bonfires, singing, dancing, and speeches are some of the traditions of Midsummer's Night. Folk traditions like kindling a fire, making wreaths, burning corn dolls or human figures made of straw, and decorating the homes, fields, barns, and everything in greenery are followed enthusiastically. Midsummer is the best part of the year when planting crops is successfully completed, and the Viking ancestors have the time to undertake battle voyages. It is a time for risk and action, and to face and counter your fears bravely. Dancing around a large phallic maypole is an important fertility ritual associated with Midsummer.

While Midsummer is the high point of the year, it is also considered to be the time of the death of Balder, the god of a sunny and happy disposition, and the start of a period that slowly inches toward cold winters.

Freyfest or Lammas or Lithasblot – July 31st–August 1st

Lammas is believed to be an Anglicized word for "hlaf-mass" or "loaves festival," a Heathen occasion of thanksgiving for bread. Heathens celebrate this festival by baking bread in the shape and figure of Freyr, followed by its symbolic sacrifice and consumption. The first of August is the time when the first fruits of harvest arrive, and in Germanic traditions, the first sheaf is offered to the Heathen gods in thanksgiving.

In today's Heathenism, Lammas (otherwise known as Lithasblot or Freyfest) is dedicated to Freyr, the fertility god, and Sif (Thor's wife), whose long golden hair is believed to symbolize the yellow fields of ripe and ready-to-harvest crops. The warriors who went to battle after the planting season returned home at this time with their battle winnings. Freyfest is the day when the hard work of harvesting and preparing for the cold winters begins.

Fallfest or Mabon – Autumn Equinox

Fallfest is a festival of joy and celebration in the Asatru calendar and signifies the beginning of autumn. It is celebrated to mark the Autumn Equinox, which occurs between September 22nd and September 24th. This festival represents the second harvest. In the Germanic traditions, community bonfires were lit, and all the home hearths were extinguished. Each family would then light their home hearths again from the community bonfire. It was a time of thanksgiving for a good harvest.

Fallfest was the beginning of gathering and saving food for the upcoming winter months. It was the day that brought people and livestock together so that everyone could spend the cold, freezing winters as a community. To be alone in the cold winters was considered dangerous, since it would mean exposure to the harsh elements and perils of winter.

From the point of view of farmers, a bad harvest would mean a long and difficult winter with the imminent dangers of famine and a shortage of food. The fear of folks not surviving the season was at its peak during this time. In present times, however, the Fallfest has little or no significance.

Harvestfest or Winter Nights – October 31st

This day marks the end of the harvest season. On this day, people would butcher the animals that are not expected to survive the harsh winters, and their meat would be made into sausages or smoked for use in the cold months. Also referred to as Frey-Blessing, Dis-Blessing, and Elf-Blessing, this festival is the time for honoring land spirits, ancestral spirits, and the Vanir gods.

It marks the beginning of winter. It is a time when everyone was expected to turn his or her perspectives from outward to inward. According to Norse traditions, the festivities of Winter Nights were officiated by the woman of the house, and the last sheaf was left in the fields for the gods, spirits, and deities.

The Winter Nights feast was celebrated by telling old tales of bravery and accomplishments and focusing on future achievements. The Harvestfest celebrated the power, veneration, and importance of our dead ancestors. Moreover, it reminded people of the important tenet of Germanic belief that death was not scary or evil. For the Nordic people, death was not as important a topic to ponder over as much as living and dying in honor.

Other Festivals and Remembrance Days in Heathenism

There are many remembrance days to commemorate multiple martyrs and defenders of Heathenism. Some of these remembrance days are given below:

January 9th – The day to remember Raud the Strong, the chieftain of a Norwegian tribe. Raud the Strong was killed for refusing to convert his faith.

February 9th – The day to remember Eyvind Kinnrifi, who was also killed for not budging from his faith.

February 14th – This day is called "Feast of Vali" in modern Asatru, and although there is no connection between Vali and St. Valentine, many modern Heathens conduct rituals and seek blessings from this god on February 14th.

March 28th – Ragnar Lodbrok's Day, the famous event of Paris's sacking by the Vikings.

April 9th – The day to remember Haakon the Great, a great defender and proponent of Heathenism in Norway.

October 9th – Leif Eriksson Day, a day to remember Leif Eriksson, one of the first Heathen settlers in North America.

November 11th – This day is called the Feast of Einherjar, on which fallen warriors and heroes in Valhalla are remembered.

December 9th – The day to remember Egill Skallagrimsson, a highly revered Heathen warrior, rune magician, and poet of the Viking Age.

In addition to these festivals and remembrance days, multiple rites of passage are also celebrated in Heathenism, most of which are community-based and family-based occasions. The various rites of passage in the life of an Asatruar include birth (name-giving ceremony), puberty, marriage (swearing of oaths by the bride and the groom), and death (funeral rites).

Chapter 10: Practicing Asatru Today

So, now that you have a fairly strong background and understanding of Asatru, it is time to answer the question, "Where to begin with Asatru in today's world?" People in the initial stages of discovering their faith or those who have been following it for some time both have a lot of questions about what defines being an Asatru today, and how to move forward in the Asatru journey. This chapter is dedicated to giving you some answers to these questions.

The first thing you must do when you get a calling to follow Norse Paganism is to just listen and talk to your gods. Remember that in Heathenism, gods are your friends and kinsfolk, and having conversations with them can build your rapport as well as help you to understand what you need to do and how to move ahead.

Talking to your gods is a habit you must foster early on in your journey. Modern life is so rife with professional and social activities that we forget to have conversations with our gods. However, if you persist in building this habit, like other habits such as eating healthy, exercising, etc., it can and will become part of your life routine.

You can find gods all around you in the form of spirits. You can strike up a conversation with any of them whenever you want. There is nothing to be afraid of. You can simply go out there and start speaking to Odin, Thor, or any of the gods you believe in. A vital element when speaking to gods is to remember to do so with respect. Initially, you will not know how and what each god expects from you during a conversation. Respect is a safe place to begin your conversation.

For example, if you need to speak to Odin, the king of the pantheon of Norse deities, then it makes sense to see him as a leader or father figure who can give you the powers of wisdom and clarity of thought. When you summon him, do so with humility and respect and seek his guidance and wisdom.

With another god, for example, Loki, you could have a different approach. While respect is a given in every conversation, with gods like Loki, you can easily take an informal approach and treat him like a friend or ally. Loki is a god who will give you what you seek but will also want something in return. So, there is a sense of give-and-take camaraderie with this god.

Another critical element about having conversations with Norse gods is to have a purpose. What do you want to ask your god? Is there something bothering you? Do you seek enlightenment, clarity, or a problem to be sorted? Casual conversations like how your day at work went should be avoided because it would be wasting the time of the gods. Remember to value the time they give you when they come to talk with you. It is important to make your time with the gods meaningful.

The second step in your Asatru journey is to collect knowledge and wisdom. Do a lot of research and learn about the Asatru faith. What does it mean? What is its history? Who are gods and goddesses? Why are they the way they are? What sets them apart from human beings? What are the roles of the various gods in Asatru?

Learn about Asatru ancestors. As you learn more about the Viking and Germanic ancestors, you will find yourself unlearning many of the elements that got incorporated into the history of the Nordic people, wittingly or unwittingly. Remind yourself that the ancestors of the Germanic tribes were highly advanced and intelligent, built fast-moving boats, and were brave warriors. They traveled long distances and conquered many lands and imbibed the culture and traditions of the conquered lands. Our ancestors could have not done so much if they had simply been savages or fools.

The more you learn about Nordic ancestors and ancient tribes, the deeper your faith will become. A great way to enhance the depth of your knowledge in the domain of Norse Paganism is to try to rephrase the books, poems, and prose you are reading and studying. Also, you could check out if translating your lessons into another language will help you. Not only will this exercise build your skills in another language, it will help you get a deeper understanding of Norse wisdom, mythology, and ancient, forgotten knowledge.

The third step to becoming a practicing Heathen is to give offerings to the gods. The offerings you give in the form of mead, wine, meats, cheese, and other foods empower the gods, and in an empowered state, they are in a better position to help you when you need them. Again, it is time to reiterate the importance of gift exchanges in Norse Paganism.

When you give a gift or offering to the gods, they return your favor multiple times because they feel empowered by your gifts. Knowing what gifts to give to which god should be part of your research and learning process. For example, Odin is a god who only drinks and does not eat anything. So, if you offer him meat or cheese or something else to eat, he is not going to be happy, and the chances of him helping you in return are slim. Mead would be the ideal offering to Odin. You can get such important information only when you keep reading, learning, and researching the Asatru faith.

The trick is to start small. Begin offerings in little bowls, create your own hallowed verses, and seek the blessings of your gods. Don't forget to talk to them and ask them if they liked your offerings. The more you talk to them, the more you will realize that your gods are continually trying to send you messages and signs in different ways and through different people.

As you gain confidence in your ability to make offerings correctly, you can slowly and steadily enhance your offerings. There are people who started with a small bottle of mead and have ended up building firepits into which they throw steaks and meats as offerings to their gods through the fire element, but don't hesitate to take those baby steps. Start now, and sooner rather than later, you will find yourself expanding in your Asatru journey.

The fourth step in your journey is to connect with more Pagans and identify yourself with a community that you are comfortable with. Although Asatru is a sort of personal religion, it is also about ancestor worship, praying, dancing, and chanting together. It is about drinking consecrated mead together, and it is about worshipping and calling on the gods as a community. Therefore, it is important that you find your Heathen kindred and become part of it.

Also, the more you connect with other Pagans, the more you learn about your faith, and the deeper your beliefs get. Being part of a kindred is immensely useful in your research about your religion. Moreover, when other believers share their experiences with you, you will realize how similar these experiences are to your own.

It gives you a sense of identity and makes you realize and accept the presence of gods and deities all around you. You are able to counter arguments about being crazy to believe in the existence of gods. You know and accept their existence without question because you know others have had the same experiences as you.

The fifth step you should follow diligently in Norse Paganism is to have fun. Again, it makes sense to be reminded that gods and goddesses are your friends and family. You don't have to pray to them to forgive your sins and cry your heart out. You can explain your problems to them as you would to a good friend or a trusting elderly relative in your family and seek their guidance and wisdom to help you scale through the problems you face.

Our gods want us to be humans and have fun, including eating, drinking, and partying. They want us to embrace our imperfections and learn from our mistakes and keep improving ourselves so that we can lead increasingly meaningful and fulfilling lives. Our gods do not call us sinners who should be punished as a form of repentance. They teach us to learn from our errors and to incorporate the lessons into our future.

Finding Fellow-Asatruars

Here are some suggestions and recommendations you can use to find fellow-Astruars in your local community or the area you live in.

The Asatru Folk Assembly is a global organization with branches and representatives found in many parts of the world. You can visit their website https://www.runestone.org/ for more information. In addition to helping you in your research about Asatru and its customs and traditions, you can also go to their "Folkbuilder" page and connect with a team member. They, in turn, can help you find someone closer to where you live.

Another Asatru community with a presence on the Internet is The Troth https://thetroth.org/. You can register yourself there if you wish. Scout under the "Find your local troth representative," and you are likely to discover an individual or group closer to your place of residence.

Get in touch with the kindred in the cities closest to you and connect with them. Most of these people will have some idea of how to help you build your personal Heathen connection. Here are a few tips to help you get started:

• Do an Internet search with the words "Asatru/kindred/Heathen, [your city name]" using different search engines. You are likely to get some results from such searches, including names, contact numbers, and addresses. You can begin with this basic information.

• Use social media platforms to find Asatru connections. Many kindred groups have a dedicated page on most of the popular social media platforms.

• You can set up a local meet group using one of the paid apps that connect with other believers. Although you might have to spend money, it could be worth your efforts. Still, you need to use this only if the earlier attempts don't work.

• Another way of contacting Heathens is to get in touch with other Pagan believers in your area, such as Wiccans. Considering that many Heathens start their Asatru journey from Wiccan beliefs, these connections are likely to help you get in touch with practicing Asatruars.

The Kindred List

Here is a small list of kindred you can connect to, learn from, or contact to find your fellow-Heathens. You can send them an email and ask for their contact details or pose your questions:

Northern Mist Kindred – Located in Oakland County in Southern Michigan, the Northern Mist Kindred is a large group of Pagans with followers from different branches of Paganism. This group is focused on improving their knowledge and wisdom about Paganism and its varied belief systems.

Kenaz Kindred – This group follows and worships the pantheon of Nordic gods and goddesses and focuses on the conservation of our planet and nature. They accept people from all cultural and racial backgrounds into their fold because they believe everyone has the right to worship and follow Norse Paganism and its gods and deities. They believe in the Nine Noble Virtues of the Odinic Rite. They are located in Eugene, Oregon.

Shieldwall Kindred – Based out of Utah, this small Asatru group's primary aim is to expand their membership, gain knowledge and wisdom, and share it with people who don't know about Heathenism and its authentic nature. This group believes strongly in the Aesir and Vanir gods, and they respect the influence these gods have on Midgard and its people.

People from all races and communities are welcomed into this group, and they do not restrict entry only to people of Germanic origin. According to their belief, their gods and goddesses traveled all over the world, and therefore, everyone should be allowed into the Asatru fold. This group is dedicated to helping new Heathens build their knowledge about Heathenism so that they can imbibe Asatru values and principles into their lives and expand their mental, physical, and spiritual capabilities.

Northern Pines Heathen Kindred – Located in Northern Ontario, this Heathen kindred believes in self-preservation and self-sustenance. They honor and maintain a deep connection with their ancestors and the Asatru community. They believe in following the kindred honor code strictly along with the Nine Noble Virtues.

They follow and celebrate the traditional Asatru feasts and festivals, organizing rituals, ceremonies, and celebrations according to each festival. They believe in and follow the Asatru pantheon of gods, including Tyr, Odin, Freyr, Skadi, etc.

Hammerstone Kindred – This kindred group is a family-friendly group and organizes trips for members and their families to areas of interest. The members meet regularly to study and discuss Heathenry topics, including lore, mythological stories, related history, and more. The members hold numerous rituals and ceremonies to honor their gods and goddesses and share knowledge and wisdom with each other.

Oath Keepers Kindred – This group was established by a group of high school friends in 2015 in Wisconsin, and they have small chapters all over the state.

Northern Rune Kindred – This Universalist Heathen kindred allows entry to all people regardless of caste, creed, race, gender, and any other distinction. The gods and goddesses of Aesir and Vanir tribes are revered and worshipped. The members strive to live by the Nine Noble Virtues as they build their knowledge about Heathenism. They are based out of Herrin, Illinois.

Wyrd Ways Kindred – Based in South Jordan, Utah, this family-oriented kindred group welcomes all who seek permission to enter the fold and come with the noble intention of learning and expanding their knowledge.

Ulfr a Aesir Kindred – Based on a strict military discipline theme, this kindred believes that it is not for everyone. They practice a mixture of Asatru, combining some old ways with the new. The group is quite orthodox in its approach. Based in Missouri, this group allows entry to people of all races, creeds, genders, and communities, but you have to prove your worth over your birth.

Hrafn and Ulfr Kindred – This group has members who follow different Pagan beliefs. Some are novice Asatruars, while some others have been practicing Heathenism for many years. The members have found their way into this Heathenry kindred from Druidic paths, Witchcraft, and Native American belief systems.

This kid-friendly kindred conducts blot ceremonies in open areas as often as possible. They are located in Topeka, Kansas.

Laeradr – This close-knit small community of Asatru is based out of a remote place in Norway. They are located on the island of Bjarkoy, an ancient territory of the Vikings. This island was a prominent region during the Viking Age and the Middle Ages. This kindred practices an inclusive, open-minded form of Heathenry and believes in human beings' deep connection with land spirits, gods, and ancestors.

There are many more such kindred groups, especially in North America. The list of Heathenry kindred is given in this book's Resources page, where you will find a more extensive list.

Worldwide Map of Asatru

The worldwide map of Heathens is a great way to connect with other Heathens too. Here is a step-by-step of how you use this map. The website link is given on the Resources page.

Open the map from the link and zoom in to your area. Even if you don't find anyone very close to your home, you will likely find Heathens within driving distance of your place of residence.

Moreover, even if you don't find anyone close to where you live, you can contact many believers (even if they live far away). They are likely to connect you with someone they know who, perhaps, lives closer to you.

Don't forget to add yourself to the map. Someone in the future might find you and seek out your guidance. This is your way of making the path of Heathenry smoother for new entrants.

If you want something badly, the universe will find a way to bring it to you. Therefore, keep your desire to become an Asatru burning through self-learning and self-development. The more you delve deeper into yourself, the more your knowledge about the external world expands. Continue your efforts to connect with fellow believers. Sooner rather than later, you are likely to meet with such people and have a great community to rely on.

Conclusion

It makes sense to finish this book with some interesting facts about Asatru, some of which have been discussed in detail in the earlier chapters.

Asatru translates to "faith," and believers extend the meaning to: "having faith in the gods." Asatru is based on an ancient religion practiced in Scandinavia as far back as the Iron Age.

It is a polytheistic religion with a pantheon of gods and goddesses who are worshipped. While there are formalities about how you pray to the gods, there are no prayers in the strict sense of the word. Each believer can seek what he or she wants from the gods in his or her own way. Gods and deities are imperfect in the world of Asatru, and they are seen as friends and advisors.

There is no prescribed scripture or dogma in Asatru. The Asatruars are continually building their knowledge and wisdom by reading *Poetic Edda, Prose Edda,* and other sources of stories. Also, archeological and historical evidence is used to understand Asatru better.

The structure of Asatru is highly democratic, with the members of nearly all Asatru societies electing their boards as well as their godi. The Nine Noble Virtues form the cornerstone of Asatru belief. These virtues include courage, truth, honor, fidelity, discipline, self-reliance, industriousness, and perseverance.

There are regular celebratory feasts and festivals and commemorative days right through the Asatru annual calendar, with the four blot rituals leading the pack.

Followers of Asatru believe in valuing nature, emphasizing the interconnectedness of everything and everyone in this cosmos. Asatruars respect nature and have dedicated nature spirits that are also given offerings and appeased if angered.

And finally, there are no proselytizing or forced conversions of any kind. Nearly all believers get an internal calling to learn about and follow Asatru.

Here's another book by Mari Silva that you might like

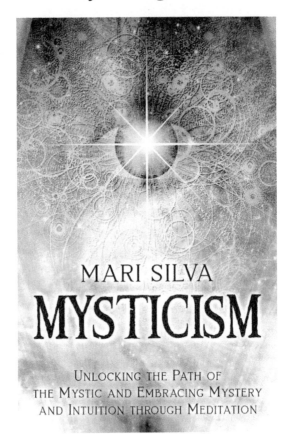

MARI SILVA

MYSTICISM

UNLOCKING THE PATH OF
THE MYSTIC AND EMBRACING MYSTERY
AND INTUITION THROUGH MEDITATION

Your Free Gift (only available for a limited time)

Thanks for getting this book! If you want to learn more about various spirituality topics, then join Mari Silva's community and get a free guided meditation MP3 for awakening your third eye. This guided meditation mp3 is designed to open and strengthen ones third eye so you can experience a higher state of consciousness. Simply visit the link below the image to get started.

https://spiritualityspot.com/meditation

References

11 things to know about the present day practice of Ásatrú, the ancient religion of the Vikings. (n.d.). Icelandmag. https://icelandmag.is/article/11-things-know-about-present-day-practice-asatru-ancient-religion-vikings

A Guide to Norse Gods and Goddesses - Centre of Excellence. (2018, October 29). Centre of Excellence. https://www.centreofexcellence.com/norse-gods-goddesses/

Heart, H. at. (2015, July 15). *Spirits of the Land: Landvaettir, Wights, and Elves.* Heathen at Heart. https://www.patheos.com/blogs/heathenatheart/2015/07/spirits-of-the-land-landvaettir-wights-and-elves/

Kindred List. (n.d.). The-Asatru-Community. Retrieved from https://www.theasatrucommunity.org/

Metalgaia. (2014, January 20). *Three Asatru Perspectives: Universalism, Folkism and Tribalism.* Metal Gaia. https://metal-gaia.com/2014/01/20/three-asatru-perspectives-universalism-folkism-and-tribalism/

Nine Noble Virtues of Asatru. (2020). Odinsvolk.Ca. http://www.odinsvolk.ca/O.V.A.%20-%20NNV.htm

Norse Holidays and Festivals. (n.d.). The Pagan Journey. http://thepaganjourney.weebly.com/norse-holidays-and-festivals.html

Norse Mythology for Smart People - The Ultimate Online Guide to Norse Mythology and Religion. (2012). Norse Mythology for Smart People. https://norse-mythology.org/

Odin's Volk. (n.d.). Odinsvolk.Ca. Retrieved from http://odinsvolk.ca/

Temple of Our Heathen Gods. (n.d.). Heathengods.com. Retrieved from http://heathengods.com/find/index.htm

Vættir. (2018, December 22). The Norse Völva. https://theheart756621753.wordpress.com/vaettir/

Vikings, Paganism And The Gods. (n.d.). Medieval Chronicles. Retrieved from https://www.medievalchronicles.com/medieval-history/medieval-history-periods/vikings/vikings-paganism-and-the-gods

Ýdalir – Inspired by the North. (n.d.). Retrieved from http://ydalir.ca/

Aettir, the three divisions of the runes- Aett. (n.d.). Tirage-Rune-Magie.net.

Aettir-The Three Divisions of the Runes & Their Use in Rune Magic. (n.d.). Www.Sunnyway.com. Retrieved from http://www.sunnyway.com/runes/aettir.html

Choosing a rune set: A beginner's guide. (n.d.). Grove and Grotto. Retrieved from

https://www.groveandgrotto.com/blogs/articles/choosing-a-rune-set

Freyr's Aett (Archive) - Ancient Runes. (n.d.). Sites.Google.com. Retrieved from

https://sites.google.com/site/mhancientrunes/textbook/section-1

HEIMDALL'S ÆTT - Marc Pugliese. (n.d.). Sites.Google.com. Retrieved from

https://sites.google.com/site/marcapugliese/chapter-6/heimdall-s-aett-1

https://www.facebook.com/dattatreya.mandal?fref=ts. (2018, July 27). 12 Major Norse Gods And Goddesses You Should Know About. Realm of History. https://www.realmofhistory.com/2018/01/29/12-norse-gods-goddesses-facts/

Instructables. (2009, December 11). How-To Read Runes. Instructables; Instructables.

https://www.instructables.com/id/How-To-Read-Runes/

Norse Religion. (2015, July 3). Norse Religion. ReligionFacts. https://religionfacts.com/norse-religion

Scribes, J. S. (n.d.). RUNES - Care, Cleansing, Empowering and Storage. HubPages. Retrieved from

https://discover.hubpages.com/religion-philosophy/RUNES-Care-Cleansing-Empowering-and-Storage

The Rune Site | Formerly Ankou's Page of Runes. (n.d.). Www.Therunesite.com. http://www.therunesite.com/

TYR'S ÆTT - Guido's Wyrd. (n.d.). Sites.Google.com. Retrieved from

https://sites.google.com/site/themindofguido/chapter-6/tyr-s-aett-1

Variety Of Rune Spreads - Celtic Book of Shadows. (n.d.). Celticbookofshadows.Wikidot.com. Retrieved from http://celticbookofshadows.wikidot.com/variety-of-rune-spreads

Your Guide to Rune Divination. (2015, October 7). Rune Divination. https://runedivination.com/your-guide-to-rune-divination/

Printed in Great Britain
by Amazon

71943148R00142